INTRODUCTION: WHO I AM AND HOW I'M GOING TO HELP YOU START YOUR FIRST ONLINE BUSINESS

Welcome, students!

You're about to take the first step towards creating your own online business in just 4 weeks, with less than £200.

This is the ultimate, condensed, step-by-step guide that will allow anyone, no matter how little experience of online business, to establish a successful online venture.

The book is designed in such a way that we break down every stage of the process into daily, bitesize, actionable segments. Making the daunting prospect of building a business plan, developing a website, marketing and promoting a business, and developing everything else in-between, seem much more manageable.

I'll be right here, every day, for 4 weeks, guiding you through every stage.

And why am I the person to do this? You might ask.

Well, I'm 34 years old. I've been establishing, running, and exiting online businesses since I was 16. From online cash management tools, to a copywriting agency, to affiliate marketing websites, right the way through to a stem cell banking business. A real diverse range of industries and business models.

Some businesses worked out well, others didn't.

The true value I'm offering in this book is my experience. My experience of what works and what doesn't. What are the fastest routes to success, what are the most cost-effective ways to market your business online, what expensive mistakes to avoid, and ultimately, what it takes to build a successful business from next to no investment.

I'm now the CEO of Vitalife Group - a group of fast-growing entrepreneurial businesses in the health and wellness sector.

I started this business shortly after I exited my copywriting agency, and put just a couple of hundred pounds into getting everything set-up. It has since generated over £1.5m in turnover, and has been profitable since the moment it was established.

So, I've been through the very process I'm about to teach you. Many times over!

I guess the next question you could ask is why am I doing this?

If I'm doing so well with my own businesses, why create a book that shows other people how I do it?

Well, the truth is, I have a real passion for business. And not just any business. In particular, I have a passion for seeing small businesses grow.

I love the excitement of building something from nothing. The 'rawness' of startups and the ingenuity and resourcefulness required to promote and grow a business without a multi-million pound marketing budget.

I want to show people who have never had their own business (or even those that have, and want to grow), how easy it is to get started. And, using my advice and guidance, how you can fast-track your way to being a successful entrepreneur by learning from my mistakes, not your own, and by focusing on the things that work.

I want to empower people who don't have a great deal of cash to invest in a business, with the knowledge and know-how to be resourceful enough to take-on established businesses and win.

Whether you already have an idea for a business, or just want to escape your 9-5 but don't know how, I'm going to help you monetise your passion, I'm going to help you plan for success, and I'm going to help you implement that plan every step of the way, until at the end of the 4-week book, you'll have a revenue-generating, profitable online business.

So, are you ready?

Let's get started.

DAY 1 - CONCEPT: HOW TO MONETISE YOUR PASSION

Tell me. Do you enjoy what you're doing right now?

Are you motivated to get up every morning and go to work? Is your job, or your current business, something that you still think positively about? Are you inspired every day to grow what you are currently doing right now?

If the answer to any of those questions is 'no', then you need to look at your passions.

What do you love to do?

It doesn't even have to be something you do as a hobby like fishing, football, playing the guitar, it could be something you feel when you go through a particular experience - like how you feel when you help someone.

That's the reason I'm motivated and inspired to create this book - to help other people to start their own business. It makes me feel good, to know that I'm helping someone.

Is it the same for you? Do you have a particular skill that you could transfer to and teach others? Are you an animal lover? Would making money from doing something that also helps animals give you motivation to keep going each day?

And, I ask you these questions because - business is tough.

Although I can teach you what's required to get a business started in just 4 weeks, with very little investment, you are still going to have bad days. Those days where nothing goes right, and you feel like no matter what you do, you aren't making progress.

Those are the days where your passion and motivation are going to be tested. And if you aren't doing something you truly love and believe in, it will not last.

I've lost count of the times I've thought of giving-up. It's easier and better-paid to just go and get a job. Go to work, 9-5, and leave all of your troubles there when you go home at night, rather than thinking about your business 24/7.

But, when the dust settles on those bad days, if you're doing something you truly love and believe in, you realise why you don't just give up. Why you don't just go and get a 9-5. Because you feel like this is your calling, this is what you were made to do. You're driven by something you can't fully explain, because you are doing something you have a passion for.

And this passion, is exactly what will drive you and your business to success.

That's why this is probably THE most important stage of starting a business. Get this wrong, and choose to pursue something for the wrong reasons, and I promise you, your business will not be around for long.

You have to understand what your passions are, and how you can make money from one or more of these passions.

So, on the first day of your 4-week start-up process, I just want you to sit and think.

Think about what you love to do, and what you'd like to focus on every single day for the rest of your life.

It could be literally anything - don't deny certain ideas because you can't see how you can make money from it just yet, we'll move onto that next. For now, just find your passions, find what you want your focus to be.

Take a piece of paper or a notebook, and jot down all of your passions.

Making money is great. And we all want more money, right?

But you don't normally make money from a business that focuses purely on making money.

Money comes from focusing on what your customers want, and delivering a product or service in a way that exceeds not only the competition but also the customers' own expectations.

So the next step is to take your passion, and think about what other people - your customers - will want from this passion. Think about how you can turn your passion into a product that customers will find value in.

Is your passion a transferable skill like playing an instrument, acting, drawing or animation? If so, this is something you can quite easily monetise through various revenue streams - blogging, vlogs, paid books like on Udemy, virtual instruction products, virtual lessons, consulting, and so on.

Or is your passion something that is less obvious to monetise, like spending time with your family and children, travelling, or other leisure pursuits - things that you'd normally pay to do rather than get paid!

There are still ways to monetise these interests - take the Sacconejoly's for instance. They created a simple Vlog around their everyday family life. Now their videos receive millions of views and they are making a lot of money from advertising and sponsorship.

It's not quite as easy to monetise interests like this, because the customer value isn't always clear - you might think, why would someone want to watch me hang around with my kids? Or watch a video of me on holiday? They don't know me, and it might be boring for them.

But, teamed with the right characteristics - if you have charisma and passion in what you are doing, and in the case of the SacconeJoly's, a little recording equipment, then you'll hook people in, and once the views start to accumulate, so will your potential to create revenue streams. It will take more time than the more obvious interests to monetise, because you need that following and awareness, but it's not impossible.

So, think about what other people might want from your passion? And from there, you can understand how you can start to make money from it.

Place all the passions you jotted down into a simple table with 2 columns - one titled 'passion' and the second column titled 'monetisation'. Don't hold back - keep an open mind and list as many potential revenue streams as you can for each passion.

Once you have all your passions and potential routes to monetisation recorded in your table, rate them.

Start with your 'passions' column, and rate them from 1 to 10 in terms of how passionate you are about each one. Then rate your 'monetisation' column on the basis of revenue potential - how realistic do the monetisation channels seem, how long will they take to materialise, and what's the top-end potential of each monetisation channel - then apply an overall rating of 1 to 10 to this too.

Finally, multiply the 'passions' rating by the 'monetisation' rating, to give each row a total score.

This will help you to deduce the passion that both carries the most importance for you personally, and also represents the best potential for monetisation.

Now you have your passion, and an idea for how you can monetise this, the next step is to form an actionable business plan on this basis.

I'll see you tomorrow for the second day of your 4-week book, to go over how we can do this, and give you examples of business plans to show you how it can be done quickly and easily.

DAY 2 - PLAN: HOW TO BUILD AN ACTIONABLE BUSINESS PLAN

So, you have your business idea. You know what you'd like to do, and how you'll make money doing it.

Now, you need to set your plan. You need to lay down your goals and objectives on paper, and you need to know how you'll set yourself apart from the competition.

A business plan can be quite a daunting thing to build from scratch - even the guides you find online can make it seem like you have a mountain to climb.

But I have a no-nonsense approach to building a solid, actionable business plan, that strips out the unnecessary fluff and focuses on the important parts, to keep the planning process as simple (and, quite importantly, as adaptable) as possible.

So, get a new Word document opened, and let's begin.

Always start your plan with your business name.

You may have thought of this already, you may not.

If not, now is the time to think about what name you'll give your business. For simplicity, it would be good to incorporate your company with this same name, so you aren't using a separate trading name - it's hard enough trying to avoid copyright and trademark infringement with one name, let alone two.

Get a sheet of paper and brainstorm some ideas. It could incorporate your own name, initials, or surname if you want it to have a personal edge, you could combine words that resemble the ethos of your business - that's where we came-up with the name 'Vitalife' by combining vitality and life.

It's good to come-up with at least 3 or 4 contenders, and I'll tell you why shortly.

Once you have a few ideas for what you want your business to be called, the first step would be to see if any of these names already exist as incorporated companies, to avoid any conflicts down the line.

It's important to note at this stage that my guide is designed for the UK market, so if you're based in the US or elsewhere, the principles remain the same, but you may have to Google the equivalent services/platforms when it comes to the links I provide.

Go to http://wck2.companieshouse.gov.uk (or your Country equivalent of a company register) and type your chosen names in the 'company name' field. This will then draw back any identical or similar company names already registered with Companies House.

This will allow you to deduce your names down to a smaller selection, removing the ones that are already registered or too similar to existing businesses that it would cause conflict or issues during registration of your business.

The next useful resource to check-out is the trademarks that are already registered under your potential business names. Now, my book does not cover or account for registration of trademarks - I feel this is something that should come later in business when you've tested your concept and can warrant the risk of investing in this intellectual property - however, checking for conflicting marks now can save you a lot of trouble down the line.

Visit https://www.gov.uk/search-for-trademark (or your Country equivalent of a trademark register) and opt to search by keyword.

Then enter your proposed company names one-by-one to see whether any other business owns trademarks of a similar nature or name.

It's important to note here that trademarks are also defined by classes - so don't be alarmed with the number of results that return during this check. Have a read of the class types at http://euipo.europa.eu/ec2/. Click on the 'Select Nice Class' and see what each class covers in terms of products and industries.

If you plan to name your company 'Widgets Ltd' and operate in the food and drink sector, then you needn't be put-off by the fact that there's a company with the trademark 'Widgets' that operates in the automotive industry, and only owns the trademark for this industry class.

So, now you should have one or two options left (hopefully the above two checks haven't completely wiped your potential names out - if they have, then repeat this process again with a new set of potential names) - choose which one to go with, and write that at the top of your plan.

Next, we need to get your mission statement down.

Your mission statement is what you set out to achieve with your business overall. This could be a long-sighted, grandiose goal of solving World hunger, or it could be something much smaller, like giving yourself financial freedom.

Don't be too worried about making this too specific, this is the 'big picture' statement - the underlying reason you want to start this business, and what you ultimately want to achieve from it.

Then, in the next section, it's time to get more specific. Create two headers, one titled Short-Term Objectives (0-12 months) and the other titled Long-Term Objectives (12 months +).

Create a bullet point list for each.

These will differ according to the business you want to establish, and where you want to go with it. But, as a bare minimum, here's what each section should always include:

Short-Term Objectives (0 - 12 months)

- Establish my business (set-up my website, incorporate the company, get a business bank account)
- Achieve £x revenue in the first year

Long-Term Objectives (12 months +)

- Achieve or exceed financial forecasts

I say every objective list should include these things because 1, without establishing your business, you have no business, and 2, without income, you also have no business.

So, these are real bare essentials for an objective list. The rest should be fleshed-out by you. Think about things like your product range (what will you offer customers, do you need to develop this or do you plan to diversify your product range), your infrastructure (do you plan to employ any staff, move to an office at some point, set up a home office), your marketing and revenue streams (do you need to establish reseller or affiliate connections to sell something, do you need to establish a connection to a PPC or advertising platform like Buy Sell Ads), and the Geography of your reach (do you plan to target International markets, if so, what do you need to do to prepare your business and website for this - translations, multiple currencies, and so on).

Now you have the backbone of your plan - these are the bare essentials that will guide you and give you direction.

The next essential part to your business plan should be your marketing plan.

Marketing is a broad discipline, it doesn't just cover how you'll advertise your products/services or how you'll get more traffic to your site, it covers the product you're offering, how it suits consumer/visitor needs, how you sit amongst your competition in terms of strengths/weaknesses, and how you can focus on your strengths in your marketing.

Again, I'll keep this part as condensed as possible so it remains quick, simple, and easy to adapt down the line - because things always change, no matter how well we plan.

Start your marketing plan with an overview of who your target market will be. Who will you be targeting with your business, what demographic will your customer-base or readership consist of. It may seem difficult at first to not just say 'everybody' - heck, everyone wants the biggest market possible for their business.

But realistically, when it comes to planning promotional activity and gearing your business towards a market, you have to aim for the low hanging fruit, otherwise, you'll be making a very expensive mistake.

When we were running our stem cell storage business, we thought we were appealing to all new parents who wanted to protect their child's future by storing their stem cells during the birthing process. But it wasn't affordable to everyone.

We spent a fortune on mass promotion to all new parents, using Facebook and Adwords promotion primarily, and it delivered very few sales. We made a big loss doing this.

Instead, if we had understood our target market more, we would have had much better results focusing on higher-income parents, with a prior knowledge of what stem cell banking is (most people don't know what the benefits of this service are, and it's a very considered purchase costing over £3,000, so it takes time and a lot of marketing money to educate and convince people without prior knowledge that this is what they need).

So, whilst it may seem silly to limit your market, it is a very essential part to your marketing plan. Who will your easiest customers be? Which customers will take the least convincing about your product/service in order to purchase? Where is your low-hanging fruit?

Specify their average age, their income level, their Geographical location, their education level, and any more characteristics you can think of, until you can picture the individual that matches all of these characteristics - and this individual is who you'll focus on in your promotional efforts, because that's where you'll get the quickest, most profitable results.

Next up is competitor analysis.

You need to understand what companies and individuals are already out there doing what you are doing. What will make you different from them?

So, start by building a list of websites and businesses that you would consider to be in direct competition with your offering.

Refer back to your target market - how can you serve this person better than anyone currently out there doing the same thing as you plan to do?

Don't be naive at this stage, you need to differentiate.

Customers/readers will already be aware of the established brands, they may have bought from your competitors before, they will be more comfortable with your competitor's brands and offerings than yours in the early stages - you'll be a stranger to them.

So, you need to offer something pretty spectacular that meets your target market's needs better than anyone is currently doing, in order to give them the confidence to choose your unknown brand over more established options.

Understand the gripes people have with your competition, read reviews on Amazon, blog comments, forums - do your research and figure out what currently annoys your target market about your competitors, and attack these weaknesses.

A great way to summarise where you sit in relation to your competition, once you've done your initial research, is to conduct a SWOT analysis. Strengths, Weaknesses, Opportunities, and Threats.

Here's how to complete each section of this analysis:

Strengths - How can you meet your target market's needs better than your competition, what advantages do you have over them? Are you more knowledgeable? Do you have access to particular resources that they do not?

Weaknesses - The reverse of your strengths. So, what advantages does your competition have over you? Do they have access to particular resources you do not? Do they have a strong, established brand?

Opportunities - With the above in-mind, what can you do to avoid your weaknesses and focus on your strengths? Is there a niche market your competition is not serving properly with their broader approach? Could you gain first-mover advantage with a particular product or service? Can you adapt your offering to address feedback from the market?

Threats - What would threaten the survival of your business and/or negate the opportunities above? Would the competition be in a position to quickly replicate your approach to better-serve your market? If so, what can you do to protect against this? Do you have particular concerns such as a lack of required funding for the business to be sustainable? If so, what options do you have if you need more funding down the line?

Next, we move on to the Marketing Mix.

From your competitor and target market analysis, here's where you'll get down on paper exactly how you'll position your 'Product' in the market, where you'll 'Place' your product/service for customers to access, how you'll 'Price' your offering, and how you'll 'Promote' your business. That's what they call the '4 P's' of marketing.

Here's how you'll complete each one in-turn:

Product - What is your product/service? What are you delivering to your target market? If it's a blog, you're offering them value of knowledge or entertainment, if it's a taught service, you're offering them value of learning something that they want to learn, if it's a physical product, you're satisfying a particular need for that product. Type here exactly what your product is, and what it delivers to your target market in the way of value

Place - How will you get your product/service/website in front of your target audience? And here, we're not asking about how you'll promote your business, this comes shortly, it's more about where your transaction or interaction with customers will take place. So, if you are planning to start a Vlog, then your main place may be Youtube, aswell as your site. If you are planning to sell physical products, then you may be considering Amazon and Ebay alongside your own site. Maybe you even plan to have a 'bricks and mortar' part to your business where you plan to open your own high-street store at some stage, or get your product/service into existing high-street stores. Type here exactly WHERE you plan to sell your product/service or interact with your target market

Price - How will your product/service be priced. This may not be completely relevant for all businesses, since some will be planning on using advertising revenue as their core income stream, and therefore won't actually be charging their 'target audience' directly. But if it's a product or a service you're offering, you need to think about how it will be priced. Will it be a premium product and therefore priced as such, or are you planning to heavily discount, at least in the early stages to break into the marketplace? Type here how you plan to price your product/service, and how this sits with current market pricing (what competitors charge).

Promotion - How will you make your product/service known to your target audience? I will go over promotional methods later in this book, and show you how to use various platforms (both free and chargeable) to promote your online business, but here we just need to summarise where we feel will be the most effective avenues to promote your business. Think about Pay-per-Click advertising, Search Engine Optimisation, partnerships with bloggers/affiliates, direct mailing (email and snail mail), social media, video marketing, newsletters, wholesale sales and so on. Type here a summary of what you believe will be the most effective forms of promotion for your business, based on the target market profile you created earlier.

This completes the basics of your business plan. We'll cover financial forecasts in a later section of the book, which should form the final part of your business plan.

So, now you have a business name, an understanding of what you want to achieve, the objectives you need to meet to achieve this, who your target market is, an understanding of your competitive environment, and how you're going to sell and promote your products or services.

Although we've built this plan, the best approach is to be adaptable. You cannot force your business model on the market, you have to adapt your model to suit the needs of the market - and often, you can't get things exactly right from the outset, no matter how advanced your plan. So let your plan change and adapt as your business develops and as you gain a greater understanding of its positioning in the marketplace.

The next step is to break this plan down into daily, actionable to-dos - that way you don't just write your plan and let it gather dust, you consistently work towards your goals and objectives by forming bitesize steps from it.

In tomorrow's section of the book I'll show you a great software to use for your to-do list, and how to formulate actionable to-dos from your business plan.

DAY 3 - TO-DOS: HOW TO REINFORCE YOUR PLAN WITH DAILY OBJECTIVES

Now you have your plan, we need to understand what we need to do, in a practical sense, every single day, in order to consistently work towards our larger goals and objectives.

By doing this, we ensure that we're always working to our plan and not deviating or losing focus.

A great software I use to formulate and manage my to-do lists is Basecamp.

I now use one of their paid options because I have so many projects going on, but they do offer a free option if you want to create just one project.

Head over to www.basecamp.com and sign-up for your free account.

Once you've set your account up, you can create your first project.

Title it the same as your business name, and then create 2 to-do lists.

One titled 'Short-Term to-dos (0-3 months)' and 'Long-Term to-dos (4 months +)'. This way we can understand which to-dos to prioritise in the short term, and we can draw down some long-term to-dos into short-term to-dos when you're in a position to action them in the next 3 months.

The great thing about basecamp is its simplicity. You can move your to-dos around very easily, comment on them, mark them as complete, edit them, and you've also got the ability (on paid versions) to invite other people to your lists, so if you're planning on employing people in your business, or working closely with freelancers and so on, the paid version can be a great, cost-effective way to keep everyone working on the same objectives and keeping track of progress on a particular part of your business.

So, now is the time to open-up your business plan and revisit your objectives.

Starting with your short-term objectives, filter out the ones that need completing in the next 3 months.

Then, break these down into what needs actioning on a practical, daily level in order to achieve the overall objective.

The perfect objective to start with is the essential one I mentioned in yesterday's book section, 'establish my business'. This is quite broad, and can include a lot of different steps, so now is the time to break this down and look at the intricate details of what needs actioning to make this happen.

When you start breaking objectives down, you'll realise that to-dos within your objectives also need breaking down themselves, to reveal even more to-dos. Don't be afraid of breaking your to-dos down to the most basic level. The more basic the to-do, the more actionable and achieveable it is, and the faster you'll be able to work down your to-do list and make progress on your business.

So for instance, with 'Establish my business' we may formulate to-dos such as:

- Set-up my website
- Incorporate company
- Set-up business bank account
- Set-up PayPal or Stripe account
- Set-up Adsense and BuySellAds account
- Set-up social media accounts
- Get logo designed

To name but a few.

Then, look at this list, and think about what needs doing for each of these to-dos in order for them to be achieved.

So, taking the 'set-up my website' to-do, you may need to:

- Purchase domain name
- Purchase hosting
- Install Wordpress
- Introduce custom theme
- Customise theme further
- Write content and upload
- Upload logo
- Install and customise plugins

So delete your original higher-level to-do of 'set-up my website' and replace with this more actionable list of to-dos that, as a whole, will allow you to meet this higher-level to-do.

Then, look at this list, and see if you can break these to-dos down any further. So following this example, take 'install and customise plugins' - this will need more specific detail to make it more actionable.

So, we may delete this higher-level to-do and instead replace with:

- Install Mailchimp plugin for email capture
- Set-up Mailchimp account

- Link to Mailchimp account
- Install contact form plugin
- Set-up email address in hosting account
- Link email to Gmail and setup on phone
- Link email address with contact form plugin
- Customise contact form to suit style of website

and so on.

Don't worry if this makes your to-do list appear huge. It's better to have a ton of actionable to-dos, than a few higher-level to-dos that have no single actionable element. You'll find yourself working through actionable, lower-level to-dos way faster than you would your higher-level ones.

I personally find it helps with motivation too to break to-dos down like this. It feels better to be able to tick-off 2, 3, 4, or 5 to-dos every day than not be able to tick anything off because your to-dos are too high-level and involve too many things in order to complete.

At this stage, don't worry if you're thinking 'but I don't know the stages involved in setting up a website' 'what's website hosting' 'what's a domain name' and so on. I have later sections of the book dedicated to explaining everything like this in much more detail - so if you know you need a website, but don't know exactly what's involved at this stage, for now just enter the to-do at a higher-level, and you can revisit your basecamp later in the book when you know exactly what this consists of, to break this to-do down into more actionable chunks.

Once you've broken down your short-term objectives as far as you can, move on to the long term objectives.

These will most likely relate to the growth of your business, so you may have plans to move to an office or a warehouse down the line, employ a member of staff, expand Internationally, and so on.

It's best to keep long-term to-dos as high-level to-dos. It's hard to predict what will happen in the longer term, and it's often a waste of time and energy thinking of longer-term plans in too intricate detail. Keeping them high-level also means that they are more adaptable.

Use the process of drawing these long-term to-dos into short-term to-dos as your opportunity to break them down to actionable, lower-level to-dos - as this means it should be happening very soon and you need to start working on the components of this to-do.

Your exact to-do lists will differ according to your particular business model and industry. You just need to spend today thinking about what needs completing to achieve your larger objectives, and when each thing needs completing - so you have your actionable, prioritized short-term list, and your longer-term list.

Now we've figured out exactly what needs doing on a daily basis to complete the objectives in our business plan, tomorrow we'll revisit our plan to formulate our financial forecasts and complete our business plan.

DAY 4 - FINANCIAL FORECASTS: HOW TO SET REALISTIC CASHFLOW AND P&L PROJECTIONS

Now we move on to the final part of your business plan, financial forecasts.

It's difficult to know exactly how your business will perform financially, especially if your business is something that is completely new to you, or may take some time to develop its revenue streams.

What financial forecasting is good for, however, is understanding what performance you NEED to achieve in order to at least survive financially. It should be used as a tool to ensure you are making enough income for the business to be sustainable - a budget, if you will.

That's why I like to start my financial forecast section with a break-even analysis. This is a great, quick analysis that will allow you to understand what the bare minimum income needs to be in order for the business to break-even ie not make a loss, and not make a profit either. Just to cover its variable and fixed costs to the point where the business can continue to operate. This then becomes your bottom-line target.

To calculate your break-even point, you first need to understand what your ongoing fixed costs (overheads) will be.

To do this, we'll kill two birds with one stone, and generate the start of a cashflow forecast for your business.

So, open up an Excel document or equivalent, and, starting in column B, type the months in the year, starting with the next full month (so if we're in August, start the forecast from September - giving you time to plan and complete this book before your business gets underway), until you cover the full year, so if you start on September, finish on August.

Then, down the left hand side, starting in row 2, enter the following:

Budget (B)/Actual (A)

Receipts (bold)
Sales
Total inflow

Payments (bold)
Cost of sales
Rent, Rates, and Utilities
Gross wages
Printing and Stationery
Professional fees and Insurance
Bank charges
Fuel and Vehicle Expenses
General Expenses
Corporation Tax

Net Cash Flow

Opening Balance
Closing Balance

For the net cash flow row, enter the formula =SUM(B6-B21) then draw this formula across all columns

For closing balance, enter the formula =SUM(B22+B24), then draw this formula across all columns

For opening balance, enter a 0 in cell B24, then in C24 enter the formula =SUM(C22+B25) then draw this across all columns

You now have a workable cashflow forecast sheet.

Now, we can start to complete our spreadsheet.

Underneath each month, because we're forecasting and working forward, in the Budget/Actual row, enter a B in each column for this row.

A cashflow forecast is a workable document that will undoubtedly differ from budgeted figures, so when we're working through our cashflow forecast and updating with actual figures, we change this letter to A, to show these are actual figures and not forecasted. But for now, they're all forecasted figures.

We'll leave sales receipts until a bit later, as this is what we can forecast from our break-even analysis, so we know exactly what we need to generate each month to survive.

So we'll move straight on to 'payments'.

Only you will know exactly what costs you will be incurring with your business - it depends on the model (whether you're going to be selling physical goods, services, advertising and so on) and it depends on your chosen business infrastructure (whether you can do this from home, or whether you need an office/warehouse and staff etc from the outset).

But the fields I've provided should give you some guidance around what overheads businesses typically incur.

Now, like with sales receipts, I'm going to ask you to ignore the variable costs here, the ones that will differ according to your sales volume and scale - and just fill out your monthly outgoings for the payments 'Rent, Rates, and Utilities' down. Also, ignore corporation tax for now and leave this blank - this isn't applicable to your first year in business since it won't become chargeable until the following year (if you're profitable), but I like to put it in there ready.

If any of the cost fields aren't relevant to your business, just enter a 0.

You may wish to use this opportunity to get some indicative quotes for things such as business insurance (we'll cover this in more detail in a later section), utility costs and so on, so we can make this forecast as accurate as possible.

Add up all of your payment fields for each column by entering =SUM(B9:B21) in cell B22, then stretch this across your other months. This figure is your fixed monthly overhead for running the business.

So, the next step towards calculating your break-even point is to understand your gross profit margin ie how much of a %age from each £1 generated is profit, after all costs of sales are considered like product/service delivery cost, carriage, and promotional expenses.

The simplicity of this calculation can vary wildly depending on your business model. If you're selling physical products, or even virtual products or reselling services of another provider, you know exactly what your cost will be per sale. You should also by now know what price you are going to sell your product/service for - following the price element of your marketing plan.

So, in this case, you then just need to consider how much you are expecting to pay in promotional fees per conversion/sale, and if there are any other costs associated with delivering your product/service to customers such as carriage.

Deduct the cost of your product/service, the cost per sale/conversion in promotional fees, and any carriage cost from your VAT-exclusive sales price, and calculate the remaining figure (your gross profit) as a percentage of your VAT-exclusive sales price by doing:

Gross Profit Figure / VAT exclusive sales price x 100 = Gross profit %age

You can find information on whether you need to register for VAT here: https://www.gov.uk/vat-registration/when-to-register (currently the threshold for registering for VAT, whether your products are VATable or not, is £83,000, so if you don't expect to turnover this amount or more in your first year, you can put-off registering for now to avoid complicating matters and obligating yourself to conduct returns).

Now you have your gross profit as a %age, you can enter a figure in your sales row, and then the cost of sales as a percentage of that sales figure.

To make this responsive and adaptable to changes in sales forecasts, enter the following sum in the 'cost of sales' row: =SUM(B2*70%)

70% was entered in this formula as an illustration, assuming my example business has a 30% gross margin. If your gross margin is different to this, then enter the remaining %age from your gross margin figure to make it up to 100%.

Draw this formula across all monthly fields.

Now, via trial and error, alter the sales receipt figure until you get a 0 in your 'Net Cash Flow' cell. This is then the sales figure that you need to generate each month to keep the business alive, and this is your monthly break-even point.

Record this figure somewhere in your business plan.

You can now lift your sales receipt figure - because after all, we want to aim for profitability - whilst still keeping this figure realistic. If you set your sales budgets too high, you'll become demotivated very quickly if you consistently miss them.

You now have a fully complete cashflow forecast for the year.

So, now you know your break even point, and you have an idea for how your cashflow will look during your first year of business, now it's time to collate the information and form some simple Profit and Loss forecasts.

To do this, open a new tab in your spreadsheet document and title it 'Profit and Loss', you can also go back to your original tab and title this 'Cash Flow' since we're now creating more tabs and its good to know what each tab covers.

So, in your new spreadsheet, enter the following in column A:

Turnover
Cost of Sales

Gross Profit

Rent, Rates and Utilities
Gross Wages
Printing and Stationery
Professional fees and Insurance
Bank charges
Fuel and Vehicle Expenses
General Expenses

Total Expenses

Net Profit

Now, it's important here to highlight the difference between cashflow and profit and loss, rarely is it identical in larger businesses - which have to take into account capital purchases (ones that don't show immediately on the P+L in one go, and are depreciated throughout a number of years, but show immediately on cashflow), stock holding (where cost of sales needs reducing each year in accordance with stock value growth - or vice versa but cashflow is still impacted by these stock purchases) and so on, but for small businesses that don't make capital purchases or hold a vast amount of stock value, then this method I'm about to show you is fine - it keeps your forecasting simple and quick.

Begin entering a formula into the Turnover field by entering =SUM(

Then click back into your cashflow tab, and select the cash inflow row throughout the entire year. Then enter a) to complete the formula, and hit enter.

This then adds all the sales revenue figures from your cashflow forecast for the year and places them as one annual figure in your turnover cell on your P+L.

Do exactly the same for the cost of sales row.

Then in the gross profit cell, enter the formula =SUM(B1-B2). This will give you your annual gross profit figure.

Then do the same as you did for turnover, on each of the cost rows.

Then in the Total Expenses cell, enter the formula =SUM(B6:B12)

This gives you your total annual overhead figure.

Then finally, for the net profit column, we need to deduct Total Expenses from our Gross Profit, so enter the formula =SUM(B4-B14)

This tells you your annual net profit figure - the money you will be left with after all things are considered (pre-tax).

The great thing about formulating your P+L from your cashflow forecast for the same year is that you only need to amend one document when it comes to adjusting figures. The P+L is now calculated automatically from the cashflow, so you only need to alter figures on your cashflow. It keeps your financial forecasting in-line and keeps things simple - which is exactly what you need, given you'll be focusing on establishing and growing your business, not spending all your time changing figures in a spreadsheet.

You can replicate what you have forecast for the next 12 months, and continue your forecasting into future years by opening and creating more tabs - so you can predict growth and cashflow performance over a longer period of time. Typically, I forecast no more than 3-years ahead. Forecasts are speculative at the best of times (noone really knows what is going to happen), and the further in the future you forecast, the more unreliable the forecasts become, so they start to lose their value or relevance after the 3-year point.

So, now you have completed your business plan - you have an idea for the income you need to generate in order to make the business sustainable, and you have some projections around financial performance.

The next step is to look at how you will collect your 'actual' financial data, and collate this so you can keep your projections up-to-date, see how you are performing in relation to your budgeted figures, and manage day-to-day accounting in the most time-efficient and cost-efficient way possible.

This is what I'll cover in tomorrow's section of the book.

DAY 5 - ACCOUNTING: HOW TO EASILY AND EFFICIENTLY MANAGE ACCOUNTING FROM THE OUTSET

Accounting is an important part of your business, if you don't keep accurate records, receipts, invoices, sales data, and process them properly, then expensive mistakes can be made.

That said, I don't regard accounting as a value-adding aspect to a business. It's ultimately a diagnostic tool - to tell you how you are performing and where improvements can be made.

Everything else in-between, the filing of statutory accounts, payroll, VAT returns, paying invoices and staff, generating invoices and recording payments, all of that takes time, and doesn't help you grow or add value to your business.

That's why it's super important to get your accounting processes in-line before you begin, and make sure that this part of your business is set-up in a way that it can record and collate the necessary information, and conduct the necessary processes, with minimal time and effort.

With the above in-mind, and assuming you aren't a trained accountant (in which case, you can probably skip this section of the book!), then you are going to need some help.

Please, do not try to save money by filing your own accounts and managing all of your accounting processes by yourself - it's time-consuming and complex, even if your business model is simple.

Take balance sheets for instance, I still don't fully understand them, and I've seen quite a few in my time. I prefer to keep things simple - sticking to P+L and Cashflow forecasts. I leave anything to do with balance sheets to my accountant - for me, they just become a black hole of time and energy, and at the end of it, even if I took the time to fully understand them, I don't see what value it adds to my business and its growth, so I'm not motivated to go through the process of trying to understand them.

Find someone that can understand it for you, and tell you what you need to know from it.

This is the earliest form of delegation you'll adopt in your business, and trust me, it is the wisest decision you'll make during the set-up and early stages of your business.

There are different levels of delegation you can take with regards to your accounting requirements, and each one depends on your level of prior knowledge and available funds - the more you outsource, the less knowledge you need, but the more funds you'll require, the less you outsource, the more knowledge you'll need, and the less funds you'll require.

When I first started, I made the mistake of trying to do it all myself, due to financial restrictions. Now, I outsource the vast majority of accounting processes to AIMS accountants for business, and use Quickbooks for my own internal reporting and records.

You can find out more about AIMS and quickbooks in the following links:

www.aims.co.uk

www.quickbooks.co.uk

So, the best way forward at this stage is to strike a balance between cost and time.

To do this, we need to first look at what's typically involved in the accounting processes of a small business, then we can see which aspects we can outsource and how we'll efficiently manage the internal aspects:

- Annual accounts (with both HMRC and Companies House)
- Annual return
- VAT returns
- Payroll
- Payment of invoices and staff
- Production of customer invoices
- Updating and upkeep of financial forecasts

These are the core accounting processes involved with most small businesses.

Run down this list now, and exclude any that will not be applicable in your particular business - maybe you don't plan to register for VAT just yet, so you won't need to file VAT returns, maybe invoicing of customers will be automated by some payment processing software you plan to use like PayPal or Stripe, so you won't need to produce customer invoices.

Once you've excluded any that are irrelevant to you, and included any that you feel I've missed for your particular business, then you have your full list of accounting requirements for your business.

I am going to recommend, based on my own experiences of these various processes and the time/effort they can take, which ones to outsource and which to keep in-house. See below:

- Annual accounts (with both HMRC and Companies House): Out-

source
- Annual return: Outsource
- VAT returns: In-House
- Payroll: Outsource
- Payment of invoices and staff: In-House
- Production of customer invoices: In-House
- Updating and upkeep of financial forecasts: In-House

As you can see, I'd opt to outsource pretty much all processes directly linked to communicating and providing information to HMRC and Companies House. These are generally the most complex aspects of small business accounts, and where, if a mistake is made, it can prove costly - so it's worth using an accountant for these.

So, once you've discussed your requirements with your accountant and decided to outsource these aspects and understand what information your accountant will need from you, then it's time to decide how you are going to handle the in-house processes as efficiently as possible, so they take up minimal time.

Payment of invoices and staff

As I mentioned, I use Quickbooks online to manage internal reporting and financial records, and if you want to do the same, go ahead and sign-up for an appropriate package to suit your business.

Then, make sure you specify to any new suppliers that you only accept invoices by email, and provide your email address to them (I'll show you how to set an email address up in a later section).

Whenever you receive an invoice, click on the '+' symbol within your Quickbooks account and click on 'Bill' - this allows you to record your invoice/bill, specify the agreed payment terms (from Proforma right through to 60 days), who the bill relates to (you can add new suppliers from this same window if they don't already exist on your software), the date the bill is being entered, what the bill is for, what payment category it falls within, and any VAT details.

You can also upload a copy of the invoice itself by attaching the file to the bill record you just created - this way you've got your official invoice records all in-line and accessible, and you may need the copy of the actual invoice when it comes to making the payment since there could be an invoice number or payment reference (or perhaps the actual bank details for the beneficiary) that you'll need to enter when making your bill payment to ensure the supplier allocates the payment correctly to your account.

I have payment runs every 10 days. So on the 10th, 20th, then at the very end of each month, I run through my 'overdue' invoices on Quickbooks for the prior period.

And yes, I said 'overdue'. Worst-case scenario is that payment is overdue by 10 days (since I run payments every 10), and its better for cashflow to pinch a few extra days on each invoice than to pay them slightly early.

It may seem that this won't make much difference, but in the early stages of a start-up, every day of extra credit you can grab, at no interest expense, should be taken!

I then pay them using my online banking account via BACS, and then mark the invoice as 'paid' on Quickbooks.

WARNING

Quickbooks is an amazing tool, and when you start utilising the 'rules' feature for common expenses, it really makes things like VAT filing a breeze (more on this shortly) - but if you're synchronising your Quickbooks account with your online banking, make sure you DO NOT consolidate your payment records ie if you're making 2 payments to the same beneficiary on the same day (and you made these as two separate payments), don't just consolidate this on the same payment record (even though Quickbooks itself encourages you to do this by allowing you to tick the invoices being paid within the same record).

Ensure that you record payments on Quickbooks individually (only consolidate the payment record if you have consolidated the actual payment to the supplier via your online banking).

If you consolidate your payment records, but make actual payments separately, it makes the 'matching' process between bank records and Quickbooks payments not correlate, and you'll end-up impacting your financial records negatively by making Quickbooks think the individual payments made on your online banking record were IN ADDITION to the consolidated payment recorded on Quickbooks directly.

Dealing with the payment of invoices in this way keeps a consistent system in-place where you know what is due when, and when it has been paid. It also means that you're only dedicating perhaps 2-3 hours per month to this activity, because you're condensing your supplier payments into just 3 payment runs per month. It's a process we call 'batching' and it improves efficiency massively.

With regards to paying staff, we pay everyone 4-weekly - I inform my accountant once a month of any overtime hours communicated to me by my general manager, and they produce the payslips for everyone. I then simply access online banking and release payment to each member of staff via BACS, delivering their payslips via email at the end of this process.

Production of customer invoices

The vast majority of our customer invoices are generated automatically on our sales platforms like Opencart and Woocommerce. Whenever a sale is made, an invoice is auto-generated from this.

That way, you have these available to-hand if you ever have an audit from HMRC or other government body, but you don't need to physically store them or generate them each time a sale takes place.

We then use Quickbooks' invoicing feature for any wholesale orders we receive, where an invoice needs manually producing.

Synchronising your Quickbooks account with your online banking account allows it to recognise when customer payments are made into your account, and recognise them as a match for the invoices that have been generated. It essentially automates the process of ensuring customers are paying their invoices and letting you know when payments are overdue and when a reminder needs emailing (you can do this with one click via the software).

VAT Returns

This is something I had outsourced until HMRC made it possible to connect directly to their filing systems via approved software - of which Quickbooks is one.

Given how easy this process now is to handle in-house, it would be foolish to pay someone else to do this.

Now, with Quickbooks' ability to apply rules to common expenses - automatically allocating a cost category, VAT status, and more to each transaction pulled through from online banking - I only have to manually verify around 90 transactions each quarter, out of 500+, then run the VAT report and hit submit. It literally takes around 1-2 hours per quarter!

Updating and Upkeep of Financial Forecasts

This happens after each quarterly VAT return that I've just mentioned. I go into our cashflow forecasts on Excel, and update the past 3 months to 'A' actual figures, then see how this impacts projections beyond this.

NOTE: Quickbooks do offer more advanced packages of their

software that will permit cashflow projections. This is something I'm currently exploring for our businesses in order to streamline the process of forecasting, but for ease of keeping my guidance in-line with the earlier advice on how to create a spreadsheet-based cashflow forecast, I'm discussing here the process of keeping your spreadsheet-based forecasts up-to-date.

It's a good time, when you've just input your actual financial data, to perhaps refresh the forecasts for the remainder of the year - making sure they remain realistic.

For instance, if you see sales revenue increasing faster than you anticipated, then increase your forecasts for the rest of the year. Or if you are consistently seeing a higher cost in one of your overhead categories, unless you can do something to bring this back within budget, then amend your forecasts accordingly - it's better to be aware of the impact this will have on your financial situation going forward than for it to take you by surprise because you refused to accept the cost is higher than you originally planned.

And that concludes my overview of accounting. I hope this gives you some insight into what's involved in this aspect of small business, and to prepare you in advance for what you need to do going forwards.

It would be a good idea to sign-up for Quickbooks and also to make contact with an accountant at this stage to discuss your outsource requirements and allow them to help with the statutory filing side of things from the off.

Tomorrow I'm going to show you how to develop your brand for next-to-no investment, based on the direction you developed in your marketing plan.

This will prepare you for the setup stages to follow, where your plan gets turned into a reality.

DAY 6 - BRANDING: HOW TO DEVELOP YOUR BRANDING FOR NEXT TO NOTHING

By now you already have your marketing mix planned. You know where you want to position your offering in the market.

And now for the fun part . . . turning that plan into a tangible brand.

A brand that will represent how you want to be seen by consumers and visitors to your site.

It's more than just a logo, it's a colour scheme, it's a typeface, it's an entire feeling and experience that immerses the customer in what you are about, before you even speak a word.

Being in retail, I appreciate how important a good brand is, and yours should be no exception - even when you're working on a shoestring budget.

That doesn't mean it's something you should do yourself either - unless you have awesome design skills already - you should most definitely outsource this to someone with experience. Your branding has to look right, and it must be professional.

It's tough enough convincing customers to buy from a completely new business even when the branding is great, so don't make this even harder.

A great resource for building your brand on a limited budget is the website Fiverr.com

On here, people from all over the World offer what they call 'gigs' for $5 each. Gigs range from someone singing Happy Birthday as a 'Jungle Man' on video, to fixing errors on a Wordpress site.

You can find literally anything in the way of creative services on Fiverr.com for next-to-nothing.

Of course, you have to be careful who you choose, make sure you select someone with a lot of positive reviews and experience, so you aren't disappointed with what they produce.

I've had a few disappointments on Fiverr before, but I've also found a number of amazing service providers that I have continued to work with - they are cost-effective and very talented. So, choose carefully, and you could find someone who you can work with in the long-term whenever you need to develop more materials or tweak your brand.

Before you contact your chosen provider, you need to communicate what you want from them effectively. Revert back to your marketing mix and your SWOT analysis - what are your business strengths? How will you be positioning yourself in the market - high-end, low-end? What are your key features and points of differentiation?

Then, try to embed this message in your branding. You don't need to map-out the entire concept of the brand to your chosen designer - that's what you will be paying them for, their creative input. But just make sure you communicate your key selling points and market positioning when you purchase your gig, so they can build something that will communicate the right message to consumers and visitors to your site.

And that concludes your first 6 days of the 4-week book. You now have a concept for your business, a full business plan with financial projections, an idea of how you'll manage your accounting requirements, and your branding is underway to becoming something tangible.

You're now ready to start building your business from your plans, and making it a reality.

Over the next 7 days, I'll take you through the necessary steps to incorporate your business, setup your website, and ultimately prepare your business for launch in the marketplace.

This is my favourite part of the business building process - where things start to become real, not just a plan on paper. I hope you'll find this next week just as exciting as I will.

DAY 7 - INCORPORATE: HOW TO COMMIT AND MAKE YOUR BUSINESS OFFICIAL

Now it's time to make things official!

In this lecture I'm going to teach you how to incorporate a Limited company with Companies House.

Again, a reminder that this book is geared for the UK market, so if you're in the US or elsewhere, then you need to find your Country's equivalent of Companies House and do a little bit of research on this beforehand.

Now, before we get things underway, you need to be aware that, just like with trademark registrations and other official processes, there are a lot of unscrupulous companies out there that prey on the complexity of these processes and try to make you pay for unnecessary services, and some are just outright scams!

So, it pays to know which companies are genuine in this domain, and which ones you should use in order to make incorporating your company as quick and easy as possible.

I'm going to tell you which company I use to incorporate my businesses, and which service level I choose from them.

Of course, you can go directly to Companies House and incorporate your company all by yourself - avoiding the fees from the company I'm about to recommend, and just paying the statutory incorporation fee of £12 directly to Companies House.

But if you do this, you'll have to generate your own, or find templates for, Articles and Memorandum of Association - the documents that outline share rights and other guidelines of ownership rights, you'll have to generate your own share certificates, first minutes, and so on.

When I incorporated my very first company at 16, this is exactly what I attempted to do. And a 24-hour process slowly became a week-long process, as I stumbled through an articles template that I had no idea whether it was relevant to my particular business or not, and tried to piece together all the other bits of information I needed to incorporate.

After that first experience, whenever I started a new company, I began using Company Formations 247 at www.companyformations247.co.uk and I've never looked back.

They make the whole process so simple, and don't try to scam you into upsells and things you just don't need. I'm not affiliated with this website or company in any way, I just find their service so quick and easy - so I've no problem recommending them to anyone looking to incorporate.

So now I'm going to walk you through the process of incorporating your new company through Company Formations 247.

Open a new browser and type in www.companyformations247.co.uk. When the page opens, you start by checking the availability of your chosen company name - but we know by now, following the name-choosing process in my business plan lecture, that our name is available on the Companies House register.

So, it's no surprise when we enter it on here, it's available for registration.

Now, at this point they will try to tag-on domain name registration - but I'd advise you to leave this for now, I have a different company I use for registering my domains - and I'll go over how to do this in a later section of this book.

So just click 'Save and Continue to Order'.

Here's where you'll see the various package levels that they offer for incorporation of your company.

And as you can see, their most basic package is only £4.99 more than the statutory filing fees incurred from Companies House themselves, so this service can be extremely cheap - depending on the service level you require.

Most of the advanced packages we can ignore, because we're using our outsourced accountant to deal with any PAYE, VAT, and filing requirements as I discussed in my accountancy chapter last week. So you don't want to pay for these services twice!

I also prefer digital records of all my documentation, so I don't want hard copy versions sending out. As far as I'm aware, it's not a legal requirement to hold hard copies of documentation (otherwise the bronze package shouldn't even be an option) - but my view is, if you ever do need hard copies for any reason, simply print your digital copies.

I'm a big advocate of the paperless office. It keeps things much tidier, and if you ever need to find a file, if you hold them digitally, then you can perform a search so your computer can retrieve the appropriate documents in a matter of seconds - that's something you can't do with a physical filing cabinet.

That's why I always choose the basic Bronze package at just £16.99 exc VAT (if you aren't going to be VAT registered from the outset, which is what I recommend unless you expect to exceed the threshold I mentioned in an earlier section, then the total cost of this package including VAT is £18.39 - so still only £6.39 over what Companies House themselves charge)

So click on 'Buy Pack' for the bronze package.

Click 'Agree to Terms and Conditions' - of course read these and ensure you are happy with them before you do so, then hit 'checkout'.

And that's as far as I'm going to take you during this section - the next steps just involve entering your payment details and other personal information and then completing your transaction.

You'll then receive an email confirming your order, and within 24 hours you'll have an email with 3 documents attached - one is your certificate of incorporation confirming that your company is now on the Companies House register, the other will be your share certificate (or certificates, depending if you are the sole owner or not), and the third is your Articles and Memorandum which outlines ownership rights.

You now have your company officially incorporated!

The next thing you should do today is contact your chosen accountant outsource, and tell them you have now incorporated your business - before you start trading you'll need them to complete a form to notify HMRC that you expect to begin doing business, and for them to register you for corporation tax.

If your accountant does not do this for you, you could face a fine from HMRC, so make sure they follow through with this registration for you.

And that concludes the process of incorporating your company.

Tomorrow, I'll show you how to create your own revenue-ready website in less than 24 hours, including domain name registration, hosting setup, and the process of choosing and modifying the design of your site.

DAY 8 - WEBSITE: HOW TO SET-UP AN ATTRACTIVE, REVENUE-READY WEBSITE IN LESS THAN 1 DAY

This is the point where your business gets its first tangible point of contact with customers - your website.

In this section I'm going to show you how to build your own website, using a platform called Wordpress, in less than 1 day and for less than £70.

You might be thinking, I have no technical expertise or I've never built a website before, surely this, combined with the fact its only costing me £70, will mean my website will look pretty terrible or won't function properly.

Not true. And it doesn't matter if you have no technical knowledge whatsoever, I'm going to be here guiding you through every single step, holding your hand, until at the end of this section you'll have a revenue-ready, attractive website live on the internet - and an email address on your new domain to boot!

I started one of our Vitalife Group businesses using this exact same setup process, and now it's generating over half a million pounds a year, and we're only 14 months on from when I launched it.

It can be done, and it can look great and form the foundation to generate some serious revenue for your business.

Now, let's get started.

First, we need our domain - this is the web address that people will type into their internet browser to land on your site.

So, open a new browser window, and go to namecheap.com.

In the main search bar, search for your chosen company name followed by .com, so yourcompanyname.com - then hit search.

If .com isn't available, don't worry, there's plenty of other TLDs you can choose from like .co.uk (if you're planning to focus purely on the UK audience), .net, .xyz and so on.

You can fit hyphens between words and see if that's available as a .com like your-company-name.com. But I really don't like this method, it's hard for people to remember, and if you really want a .com TLD, it's better to just get more creative - for instance if your company name is John Smith Ltd and you're going to build a blog and brand around yourself and what you do in your day-to-day life, then you could search for the domain www.adayinthelifeofjohnsmith.com - yes it's a bit long-winded, but it's memorable. And, other than direct referrals where your web address doesn't really matter, with word of mouth referrals and direct visits from people entering your address in the URL bar, it HAS to be easy to remember.

Once you've found your chosen domain name, click the cart button to the side of it, and then follow the account setup and purchase process. Remember your login details for this account as you'll need them later to set the hosting up and take your site live on this domain.

Ignore any upsells for hosting or whoisguard (unless its free) from Namecheap, I have another source for hosting that I use for Wordpress sites.

Now you own your domain name, you need to purchase and setup your hosting, so you can install Wordpress and start to customise and build your site.

For hosting Wordpress sites, I just use Hostgator's shared hatchling plan - unless you're expecting masses of traffic from the outset (and you really shouldn't when we're working on a £200 setup budget), it's a perfect, low-cost way to get started.

So, go to hostgator.com and click on Web Hosting, then click the Sign Up Now button for the Hatchling plan.

Click the tab 'I already own this domain' then proceed to complete the field with your exact domain name you just purchased on namecheap.

Now, the billing cycle tab is where you need to decide what's best for you, the longer you commit for the cheaper the monthly cost but the higher the initial outlay, the shorter the commitment, the more expensive the monthly cost, but you only have to pay this month-by-month. So, assess your own needs, do you see your business as a long-term plan, and I hope you do - then if so, and if you can afford the initial outlay, go for one of the better value, longer-term packages.

What you choose is entirely up to you here.

Then, proceed to complete your other account details and complete the transaction and account setup process. Again, remember the details you enter here as you'll need to access your account shortly to set your site up.

Once complete, you should receive an email from Hostgator with your Cpanel (or Control Panel) and billing account login details, along with details of which URL to visit to log into your accounts.

Next, you just need to point your domain name to the hosting provider's nameservers. So, revert back to namecheap and login.

Find your domain within your account, and click 'manage'. Under the 'domain' tab for your selected domain, scroll down to the 'nameservers' section, and select 'Custom DNS' from the drop-down menu, then revert back to your account info email from Hostgator, which also includes your two nameserver addresses - paste these in, in the same order. You've now just pointed your domain to your hosting.

Now, we want to install Wordpress on our hosting, so click on your Control Panel link in the Hostgator email, and enter the details from the email to login.

Scroll down to software and services, and click on 'QuickInstall'.

Then click the 'Install Wordpress' button down the page.

Select your domain and complete the install process.

Once installed, you will receive a confirmation email, with your login details and admin URL for your Wordpress account.

Now, we want to find a good theme for our new Wordpress website. I recommend themeforest - an Envato site.

Open a new browser and go to themeforest.net.

This is now where you need to fully understand what your website will do. Will it be a storefront where you'll sell physical products, will it be an information-based site with a page that sells various services, will it be purely information-based and sell advertising space, or will it be a blog or vlog?

If you choose the right theme, you can quickly and easily adapt it to suit your requirements, but choose the wrong one and it will be a very long process of editing and probably getting developers involved to make it how you want it.

You need to find a theme as close to how you want your finished website to look like from the off - that way minimal work is required to customise and make it yours.

In the search bar, search for something related to the theme you want on your site - so if you're building a food blog, search 'food blog', if you're planning to build a vlog search 'video blog', a magazine search 'magazine', an ecommerce site then search 'ecommerce (and the industry you want to operate in)' like 'ecommerce fashion'.

It might take quite a few searches and some trawling to find the one you want, but you should be able to find something on themeforest - it's one of the biggest collections of Wordpress themes online.

Once you've found the one you want, click 'Buy Now' under a regular license option. then complete the account setup and checkout process, and you'll be given access to the theme as a download ZIP file.

Download the file when you get to this stage, and then return to your Wordpress login URL, provided to you on the setup confirmation email. Enter your login credentials, then go to 'Appearance' on the left-hand menu, and select 'Themes'. Then when this page loads, click the 'add new' button, then 'upload theme' and then browse for the file you downloaded from Themeforest, and select for upload, then click 'install now'.

Once installed and selected, you'll be able to visit your domain to see how this theme looks and to ensure it all displays as it should.

Then, we move on to customise the site. Start with 'Theme Settings' - the options here depend on the particular theme you install, so it will be a case of just going through and filling each field one-by-one as necessary. But this will typically cover the header logo (which you should have by now from your Fiverr provider who you tasked with designing your branding), Favicon (the little icon that shows in the browser tab), settings such as what is displayed and what isn't (social links, menus, and so on), and other settings.

Once you're happy with your customising of the settings, go to the 'customize' link under settings and in here you'll be able to make changes to the colour scheme, and also specify the widgets to show on your site (if you don't already know, widgets are ultimately features that you can include, customise, and display on your site - examples can be an email capture form, advertising blocks, archives, categories, more menus, and so on).

Once you've done what you need to do here, you need to set-up your website menu - so the links that people will be able to click on to access the various parts of your site.

Start by clicking on 'pages' - and in here you can create your pages and fill with the necessary content. For things such as embedding contact forms and other interactive features on your pages, you should install the appropriate plugin first (more on these in a minute), and this will generate some shortcode for you to enter on your page for this to appear on your site. But for now, just create your pages, and fill with text/image content - we can revisit interactive features after the plugins have been installed.

No need to create a Home page, as most themes will include this as default.

You may want an 'About' page, giving readers more background information about you or your business, a 'Services' page, where you'll list your services and introduce PayPal payment buttons for people to purchase these online, a 'Contact' page for people to get in-touch.

The type and the amount of pages you produce will depend on the type of website you're building. You may want to also produce some terms and privacy statement pages for the footer of your site whilst you're generating your other pages - it doesn't matter if you want these in a different location on the site, this is just where you create your actual pages, your menus, and their location, will be where you provide the link to these pages.

Then, when you've created all your pages, revert back to the 'Appearance' and 'Menus' tab.

Again, what you see here will vary slightly depending on your theme, but typically you'll see two tabs - 'Edit Menus' and 'Manage Locations'. You may wish to bring with the 'manage locations' tab to check which menu displays where, then revert back to the 'edit menus' tab to change what is displayed in this particular menu.

You'll see down the left-hand side it shows the pages that are available to link in this menu, tick the ones you want in here, then click 'Add to Menu'. This will then draw the pages across, so you can organise the order in which they are displayed by clicking and dragging/dropping.

When you've done with your menus, hit 'save menu' at the bottom of this page, and check the front-end of your site to ensure it all displays properly and the links work.

So, by now you have a custom site, pages, some content, and a menu. You're almost there.

Now, we move onto Plugins. These are great add-ons that simply 'plug-in' (hence the name) to your existing theme and site, and add extra functionality and features. Most are free to download/install, and have premium upgrades if you want more advanced features - so you can generally find a plugin to do what you need it to do for free, without the need to upgrade.

Now, I'm going to recommend some great plugins that I use on almost every Wordpress site I build - no matter what the concept, ecommerce, blog, whatever.

Contact Form by Subsystic - a great and easy-to-use contact form plugin that allows you to produce and customise the appearance of your contact form, then generate a piece of shortcode that you simply copy/paste into your contact page for this to display

Mailchimp for Wordpress - if there's one thing that holds value for any site, it's the ability to capture data from its visitors, and use that to remarket your products/services/website to them. Grabbing their email address by offering them something of value to download can be a great way to do this.

Set-up a Mailchimp account by going to mailchimp.com - they are free for up to 2,000 subscribers or 12,000 emails per month, then from within your account set-up a new list of subscribers, then go to Account > Extras > API Keys, then click on 'create a key' when it generates, copy this key - it's all you'll need to link to your Mailchimp for Wordpress plugin so you can feed subscribers directly into this account.

I'll cover more on Mailchimp management and the sending of emails on this platform during Week 3 of this book.

Once you've got this plugin operational, think of what you want to offer to your visitors that they'll find value in. For me, on gavinedley.com, I offer this particular section of the book for free in return for an email address - via a hidden Youtube video I uploaded that you can only access with my direct link.

This was easy to set-up in terms of the Mailchimp plugin, because it's just a link - I don't need to deliver anything on an email to the new subscriber, or do anything manually. I just set the 'success' message on the plugin settings to provide the hidden Youtube link to the new subscriber. They then click the link and get what I promised, and I have captured the email address so I can remarket the full book to them on Udemy.

These are my two essential plugins for any Wordpress site.

Any other functionality you need will probably also be accessible via a plugin - just search, install, activate, and play around with the settings to get them to deliver what you need.

Need PayPal integration, there's a plugin for that, need Stripe integration, there's a plugin for that, need Buysellads space, there's a plugin for that, need Adsense ad placement, there's a plugin for that. Basically, anything you need, there will more than likely be a plugin for it.

And if not, and you need something custom building or resolving on your site, then revert to the resource I showed you before for your branding - Fiverr.com. There's some hugely talented developers on here who will happily help you for a small fee, just do a search for what you need.

And that concludes the basic foundations of your Wordpress site - where you take it from here will depend on the type of site you're wanting to build - if you are building an ecommerce site, you'll want to go into your Woocommerce area and start completing information and adjusting your settings here to set-up your products on the site, and adjust shipping charges/locations and so on. If you are building a blog, you'll want to probably begin your first post to populate the site with a little information, which you can do via the 'Blog Posts' tab. And so on.

One final area I want to cover in this section, now your hosting is up-and-running, is email addresses.

Go back to your CPanel, and click on 'Email accounts'. Here, you can create your own email account on your new domain.

Enter the email address you want, your password, and then select unlimited mailbox quota, then 'create account'. The account will then show in a list below the account generator.

You can now access this address via webmail by typing yourdomain.yourtld/webmail and entering the email address and password you just used to create the account.

No doubt though you will want to use this address via a client such as Outlook or Gmail - I use Gmail for mine, just so I can access from anywhere with an internet connection.

To find the setup instructions and details for this, click on More > Configure Email Client from your list of email addresses, and follow the guide.

You may now wish to link this email address with your contact form plugin or display it on your contact page for people to get in touch via this new address.

And that's your website and email all setup, next, I'll show you how to prepare your product or service for the market.

DAY 9 - PREPARE YOUR PRODUCT/SERVICE: HOW TO GET YOUR PRODUCT READY FOR THE MARKET

By now, you have your brand and your website to showcase what you have to offer.

Something we haven't covered yet, however, is preparing your product/service for the market. The level of preparation involved will depend on your particular business model and revenue channels.

If you plan to build a blog, your product is your content, which you'll have to plan, develop, and schedule for release so that you are delivering a constant flow of new posts for your readership.

If you want to build a Vlog, then the same principles apply as for a regular blog - your content is your product. But you may also need to invest in some recording equipment, microphones, a backdrop, camera stand, and so on - to make sure your product is high-quality and not disregarded by viewers due to lack of credibility or poor quality.

If you are building an ecommerce site, you have your sales platform, and you know what you want to sell and what price you want to sell them at from your business plan, but have you made contact with suppliers? Do you know the extent of the initial range you want to offer? Sit down and choose which products you will offer from your suppliers' catalogues.

If you are offering services such as consulting or management services, do you have everything in-place such as the necessary documents, contracts, software, and other products that will allow you to do your job for your clients.

If you are selling digital products such as e-books or e-books, have you already built your book? Is it in download-ready format? If not, you need to build your product and make sure it is deliverable to customers.

Whatever your product/service, a great exercise to complete at this stage is to build a 'customer experience flow'.

This is not a business school model, it's something I just like to do when starting a new business, to fully understand the customer's perspective of my offering, and to ensure I have everything in-place to fulfill their needs with my product or service before the business launches.

This isn't a planning exercise, as we did this during our marketing plan - understanding our target audience and how we'll satisfy their demands with our product or service. This is a more practical exercise to ensure everything is in-place before you begin trading.

Some customer experience flows will be much simpler than others - depending on your business model.

So, to begin building your flow, you need to think about every point of customer contact. Every moment where they interact with your product/service and your business as a whole.

So, using Ecommerce as an example:

- Customer visits the site
- Customer puts items in cart and follows checkout process
- Customer receives confirmation email
- Customer receives email notifying them of despatch
- Customer receives goods
- Customer uses goods
- Returns process

So, now we think about what's involved at every stage and what the customer experience of your product will be like:

- Customer visits the site and follows checkout process

So, we already have our site. But is it easy to navigate, does it all function properly (have you tested it thoroughly), and is it user-friendly?

- Customer emails

Do you have these set-up? These are default settings in Woocommerce, but have you customised the emails? Have you tested they get delivered okay? Have you customised the content? What delivery service will you be using to send your goods? If tracked, will you want to hook-up the tracking info to the despatch notification email to limit customer enquiries regarding the progress of deliveries? Check for a plugin that may do this and create the connection to your courier platform.

- Customer receives goods and uses them

Do you have the correct packaging and tape ordered and ready so the goods can be sent safely and cost-effectively? Do you have a printer and plenty of ink/toner for the packing lists? Will you be sending out flyers or promotional content with orders, if so, you need to order these in advance of trading. Will you be requesting feedback from customers to build a customer service rating that you can advertise on your site like Feefo or other independent service? If so, this needs setting-up and integrating - check for appropriate plugins. ill you be completely outsourcing your fulfilment to a fulfilment warehouse? If so, you need to establish that contact and account, and familiarise yourself with their order management plaform. You'll also need to establish some understanding of how orders will be fed through to them - will you use an API connection (a direct, automated connection to their system from your website) - in which case you'll need help from developers, or will you begin by supplying them a CSV file of orders on a regular basis?

- Returns process

What is your returns process? Will you cover return shipping? How will you cover it, reimbursement or prepaid shipping labels (common with clothing goods)? If using labels, you'll need to set a returns service up with a courier and get the necessary hardware to print these and send out in orders.

Thinking about the customer experience in micro-detail like this ensures you have everything in-place to deliver your product or service before you start trading - ensuring the customer experience is positive from the outset, and you don't have any unexpected issues with your product or service.

Now you know you're all set in regards to your product or service, now we need to look a little deeper to ensure we have the appropriate infrastructure in-place to support the delivery of this product or service, and to sustain the business.

This is what we'll look at in tomorrow's section of the book.

DAY 10 - INFRASTRUCTURE: HOW TO PREPARE TO SERVE CUSTOMERS EFFICIENTLY AND WITH GREAT SERVICE

So, you now have your website and your product/service is ready for the market.

Now is the time to ensure that your business infrastructure is equally prepared for trading to get underway.

Your company infrastructure will differ wildly depending on your business model. For bloggers and vloggers, the only infrastructure you need is a computer, an internet connection, and other relevant equipment to deliver your content like microphones and a video camera etc.

For an ecommerce site, the infrastructure will be much broader - you'll need space to store your goods, a streamlined process for fulfillment, an appropriate method of taking-in new deliveries, a returns process and so on, and even if you are outsourcing fulfillment to a dropshipper or fulfilment house, you still need to think about how this is going to be set-up - will you use an API (a direct link to your supplier so orders are transferred over automatically), a CSV file via FTP (similar to an API, but the supplier would actively have to pick this CSV file up from a destination on your site each morning to fulfil your orders), or will you send orders over manually via email?

At this point, a good exercise is to revisit the customer experience flow you explored yesterday to ensure your product or service is ready, but this time view this flow from a more internal perspective.

There will be some crossover from your thoughts yesterday, back-end processes directly affect how the front-end of your business performs and delivers its products or services to customers, but now is the time to seek out those processes completely hidden from the customers' view - to ensure these are equally prepared for your business to get underway.

So, how are you processing payments for your revenue streams? If PayPal, have you confirmed all of your details and lifted your withdrawal limits in advance of trading? There would be nothing worse than trading getting underway, only to realise you are restricted to withdraw just £1,000 per month from your PayPal account - that could throttle the cashflow of your business before you've even got going properly.

What about your phone line and broadband? Do you have solid, appropriate utilities in-place and ready to go? If you're having a phone line, are you taking orders on the phone also? If so, who will answer the phone and take these orders, and what process will they follow? You need to ensure when taking card payments you follow a PCI compliant process, or you could face a large fine, so read up on this first at pcisecuritystandards.org and take a look at their Standards Overview page where you'll find a self assessment questionnaire on meeting these.

If you're using PayPal pro or handling card transactions directly on your website, then you'll also need an SSL certificate for your site, and you may need to check PCI compliance on this process too.

If you're selling a software or digital product, does it have the necessary protection in-place such as the generation and use of registration keys and so on, so you are protecting your product and business from piracy.

So, as you can see, your business infrastructure, and what you need to be in-place before you begin trading, can vary depending on your business model.

Take the time now to go through all of your business processes with a fine tooth comb, examining every minute detail, to ensure your infrastructure is robust enough to deal with a whole range of scenarios and situations, even those beyond your daily business activities. Trust me, things never go completely to plan, so it pays to have contingency plans in place for your infrastructure in case something goes wrong, so it doesn't stop your business from operating completely.

We've worked with numerous suppliers and fulfillment centres in our ecommerce businesses, and sometimes those relationships break down, or your suppliers cease trading - you need to prepare for these situations so you know how you'll continue to serve your customers if this happens.

It may seem like wasted time, given all you are wanting to do now is get your business launched - but trust me, it will save a lot of time and stress later down the line when something does go wrong. It pays to plan in advance for these situations so you can act quickly if they do occur.

So that covers your business infrastructure. Once you've completed the above exercise, you should be confident in the knowledge that you have everything you need in-place to support the delivery of your product or service to customers, and to ensure your business continuity.

Next up, I'm going to teach you a few cashflow tips that you can apply from the very early stages of your business, to ensure you can setup and continue to grow with very little investment.

DAY 11 - BOOTSTRAP: CASHFLOW TIPS BEFORE YOU BEGIN

Cashflow is key to any business. A business could be massively profitable, but if it doesn't have the cashflow, it will crash - no matter how big or profitable that business is.

Now, scaling that concept back to a start-up, cashflow becomes even more important. You won't have the profit or the trading history to convince banks to lend, and it's difficult to convince angels and Venture Capitalists to invest on the back of something with no market proof - especially if this is your first business and you don't have an experienced management team in-place.

So, the only real source of cashflow for most start-ups is the initial start-up capital from the owner, and the income it generates, and trying to scale a business, making necessary investments for long-term growth, and taking-on necessary growth projects that may or may not fail, whilst remaining cashflow positive, is a huge mountain to climb and a very thin line to walk.

It's probably going to be your most difficult challenge as you start your business and as it starts to grow - I know it was mine.

So, given its importance, it's imperative you do everything you can to maximise your cashflow right from the outset of starting your business.

There's ultimately two ways to maximise cashflow, reduce or

delay outgoings, and increase or speed-up incomings.

Starting with the former, here's a few tips on how to reduce or delay your outgoings (again, the relevance of these will depend on your particular business model - take from them what are applicable to you and your business):

- Shop around for the best deals
- Always ask for trade discounts from suppliers (not many retailers work on standard trade prices, and you'll be working to a disadvantage in comparison to the competition if you do)
- Be cheeky and ask for the longest payment terms possible, start at 90 days and work backwards negotiating with them
- Prioritise supplier payments and choose who gets paid on-time and which payments you can safely pinch a few more days or weeks on without impacting your business
- Try to secure Sale or Return or consignment arrangements if you are going to be holding and selling stock, so you aren't stuck with money invested in stock that doesn't sell through quickly
- For capital and equipment purchases like recording equipment and computers, try to secure interest-free payment plans so you can spread payment over several months without extra charge
- Take advantage of free trials for software, even if you plan to buy them anyway, get your first 30 days for free and that's 30 days where you can generate income without spending anything on that particular software for your business

Then, looking at the increasing or speeding-up of incomings, here's a few ideas:

- Maximise and diversify your revenue streams (if you're doing ecommerce, can you charge the brands you are selling for promotional placements on your site or generate cash from selling advertising space, if you have a blog, could you charge brands for product placement in one of your posts, and so on - don't just rely on your primary income stream)
- Minimise your own payment terms to customers. Work on pro-

forma where you can (payment up-front) and minimise payment terms elsewhere where you have to offer them. If your business is mainly wholesale, then it may be worth exploring invoice factoring with a finance provider so you can get the funds immediately on production of invoice rather than waiting for the term to expire

- Search for grant funding and business support in your area. We once received a non-repayable grant for £2,000 for a website and an additional £500 seed funding from TATA's Steel Enterprise scheme for one of our businesses - so it's worth having a search to see what you're eligible for

- Explore advertising channels that are commission-based or take a fee on completion of a sale. Examples can be Amazon, Ebay, Etsy, ODesk, affiliate marketing and so on. This means you won't be incurring advertising expenses until income is generated from that advertising channel - it's a low-risk form of advertising, and that's exactly what you need when cash is tight - you can't afford to blow money on testing different advertising channels at this point to see what works and what doesn't

There's plenty of other ways you can maximise your cashflow, and these are just a few techniques that I use in my businesses.

Keep on the right side of cashflow throughout your setup and growth, and you'll have tackled the biggest challenge that most start-ups face.

On the next book section, I'm going to show you how to research the legalities of operating in your chosen field, and how to ensure you stay on the right side of these.

An admittedly boring, but essential part to setting up your business.

DAY 12 - LEGALITIES: WHAT YOUR LEGAL REQUIREMENTS ARE, AND HOW TO STAY COVERED

Boring! I know. It's the last thing you want to be spending time doing when you're going through the exciting process of setting up your business - you'll probably now be itching to start promoting your new site and products or services to get your first customer.

But, don't rush this. I've been through this process many times, and even now, I'm just as eager to get my new businesses to market as I was with my first - but now I have the discipline to ensure every avenue is covered and not to rush through or ignore the 'boring bits'.

These checks are very essential to the continuity of your business - and when you've committed to long-term overheads, and you're relying on the income your business generates, the last thing you want to happen is for it all to come crashing down because you've suddenly discovered you're breaking the law in some way or you've exposed yourself to a lawsuit.

One of my businesses when I was younger was importing and

selling teeth whitening kits. It was, and still is, a hot market - everyone wants bright white teeth, right? You see the 'whitening' selling point attached to almost all toothpastes and mouthwashes on the market now.

I got into this following personal interest, and a frustration that dentists were charging extortionate amounts to apply bleaching gel that is, effectively, very cheap and completely safe to apply yourself provided you follow some simple guidelines.

So I sourced a manufacturer of teeth whitening kits through alibaba.com and I imported my first batch. I began selling on Ebay, and sales took-off immediately. I did this alongside a job I took after University that paid around £26,000 a year, and quite quickly, my earnings from my teeth whitening side business were generating almost 4 times the amount I was earning in my job. Granted, this was turnover, but even so, on a 25% net margin, I was near on doubling my annual income with this business, and at 21, a £50k+ wage was pretty good going.

Until one day, I received a number of emails from Ebay, stating they had pulled my listings for violating their terms - I had illegal products listed.

At this point I was forced to look further into the legalities of teeth whitening, and discovered that there was a legal restriction in the UK to sell carbamide peroxide gel that was up to 0.1% in strength. The strength I was selling was 35%!

Now, 0.1% would do absolutely nothing in the way of making your teeth whiter - it was basically, I feel, a way for the dental association to monopolise this area of the market by ensuring that the stuff you could sell legally at retail simply didn't work, and to get true results, and a stronger carbamide peroxide, you'd have to visit a dentist and pay their extortionate fees - which was exactly why I started my business so that people could avoid this.

I'd jumped the gun. I became too excited about the income I was generating from the product, that I failed to properly research the legalities, and now not only had my business lost its access to its marketplace - Ebay, I also had money invested in stock that I couldn't sell, and if I did, then I could face criminal prosecution with the maximum penalty being up to 6 months in prison.

Suffice to say, I quickly exited the teeth whitening business, and moved on - but it was an expensive mistake to make. As I said at the start of this book, I want you to learn from my mistakes, not your own - and this is one important lesson I'd like to teach you, research the legalities of your business before it gets started.

Again, as with all of this book, because of the broad range of businesses I'm covering, the extent to which you need to research legalities and protect your business will very much depend on your business model - but here's a list of checks that may or may not apply to your particular business:

- Is your product/service legal to sell in your chosen territory (obviously, laws change from Country to Country, so if you plan to sell Internationally, you have to check local laws in each territory)
- Do you have appropriate liability insurance in-place (public liability, employer's liability, product liability, professional indemnity, and so on)
- If you are selling food/drink items and fulfilling in-house, do you meet all hygiene standards imposed by environmental health. You will also need to register with your local authority so they can conduct visits to your premises
- Are your payment processes PCI compliant? I mentioned this in an earlier section and where you can visit for advice
- Do you have traceability of the goods you're selling to customers? ie can you record batch codes when stock comes in, and then attach this batch code to particular customer orders for that item. So if a product recall occurs, you can trace items back to individual customers
- Do your website terms and conditions also follow mandatory

trading conditions like the distance-selling regulations and cooling-off period?

- How will you be storing customer data like email addresses, and does this fit with your privacy policy or statement? Is it in-line with GDPR requirements?

- Do you need particular licenses or authority to sell your product or service? Like being registered with the FCA if you're in financial services and so on

- Are you accounting for VAT in your pricing to customers? If your products/services are VATable, but you aren't planning on registering from the outset, it's sometimes good to incorporate the VAT mark-up on your goods anyway, so you know what you would have to charge inc VAT if you reach the threshold for registering sometime soon. That way it's not a nasty surprise for customers to see a 20% increase in your recent pricing when you register

All of these things may not be applicable like I say, however some will, and there will be others I have missed too - this list isn't exhaustive. It depends on the industry and markets in which you plan to operate, and your business model.

Just take some time today to research all your legal requirements, and ensure you plan and put things in-place to ensure you remain on the right side of the law and other regulations as you begin to trade.

On tomorrow's section, the final part of the setup module, I'll show you how to put measures in-place to protect the downside. If everything goes wrong, and your business fails, what can you do to protect yourself to ensure you're able to pick yourself back up and try again.

DAY 13 - PROTECT THE DOWNSIDE: HOW TO LIMIT YOUR RISK

Sometimes, no matter how hard we try - things just don't work out.

It's happened to me multiple times, some of my businesses have failed, and unless you are extremely lucky, it will probably happen to you at some point too.

It's an occupational hazard for the entrepreneur.

What smart entrepreneurs do, is protect the downside of failure - ensuring they can pick themselves back up after it happens, and try again at something else. Or even at the same thing, with a different approach.

So, what does 'protecting the downside' consist of?

It can take all sorts of forms, but it's ultimately about creating a safety net, and contingency plan, for if the worst case scenario happens.

If you run out of cash, and can no longer pay suppliers or your rent, what can you put in-place to minimise the damage to you personally?

Large companies often place their assets in a holding company, and have a separate trading entity, that effectively leases the equipment and/or property from the separate holding company. That way, if anything was to go wrong with the trading company, the assets wouldn't be seized, as they belong to a separate entity.

That's a pretty complex setup, and you'd have to have a good deal of assets to be worth paying the legal fees to set all of this up properly - so we won't be going this far in this book.

Instead, think about your personal situation. Are you going to continue working or taking a wage from elsewhere whilst this business becomes established? If you're going to take the leap and leave employment to pursue your business, can you quite quickly and easily find another job with a similar income level as the one you left? So you can still afford to pay your personal bills, your rent or mortgage and so on.

It's about running through scenarios in your mind, to ensure you have a financial safety net in-place should things not work out with your business.

If the set-up of your business involves the purchase of capital equipment such as computers, machinery, hardware and so on, can this be quickly and easily liquidated ie re-sold, with minimal reduction in value from the purchase price? That way you could pay your debts by liquidating the business.

If the equipment you are considering purchasing is difficult to re-sell or depreciates rapidly, then consider a lease arrangement instead, at least initially until the concept of your business is proven and you achieve financial stability.

Or perhaps, rather than loan your business the money it needs to get started and record this on your director's loan account, you could purchase the equipment and assets that your business needs personally, then lease it to your business - so the assets are owned by you personally. There are, of course, different tax implications with restructuring purchases like this, so it would be worth speaking with your outsourced accountant for some advice on this first.

The fact that we have already incorporated your company as a separate legal entity, and that all trade will be conducted through this entity, is one of the best ways to protect yourself personally from any creditor. However, it doesn't negate all risk or legal responsibility - as a director of the company you can sometimes still be held legally responsible, depending on the circumstances, so it's good to explore these other measures and damage limitation techniques, should the worst case scenario occur.

And that now concludes the 'setup' week of your book. By now, you have a fully-operational, revenue-ready website, your product and business infrastructure are prepared for the market, and you've done the necessary research and contingency planning to ensure the continuity of your business - you're now ready to start promoting your business and website, and to start trading!

In next week's module, I'll teach you all about promoting your website and products/services in the most cost-effective ways possible, from social media, to video, to emailing, to PPC and more.

Next week, we'll hopefully net your business's first customer. Are you ready? Let's go!

DAY 14 - SOCIAL MEDIA: GET THOUSANDS OF FOLLOWERS AND LIKES FOR LESS THAN £50

Social media, these days, is as broad as you make it.

We have the proven, long-standing platforms like Facebook, Twitter, and Instagram, then we have the more specific platforms like LinkedIn for B2B and professionals, then we have platforms like Pinterest, Tiktok, Youtube, Foursquare, Snapchat, Triller and so on.

Social media has become so broad that it's a confusing and rapidly-changing area of marketing to delve into, you could spend several days just researching what the various platforms are actually used for.

I find the best approach is to focus on the 3 highest traffic platforms - Facebook, Twitter, and Instagram, and then perhaps throw-in a couple more accounts that are relevant to your particular business. So if you're a blogger or vlogger, you'll want a Youtube and a Vimeo account, if you're a consultant or someone selling teaching materials, using Instagram Live and Facebook Live could be useful ways to promote your teachings and invite live feedback and questions from viewers.

So, today I want you to research the various social media platforms and choose at least 2 others, relevant to your business, that you'll use alongside Facebook, Twitter, and Instagram.

Then, set-up your profiles using the branding materials provided by your Fiverr designer, and link your social profiles to your website, then create social links on your website to your various profiles (if your theme doesn't have this built-in by default, there are plenty of plug-ins available that you could use for this).

Now you've chosen your accounts and set your profiles up, I'm going to show you how to build a genuine following rapidly on both Facebook and Twitter, for next to nothing.

Your following is your audience, the people who like your Facebook page or follow your Twitter profile. A large social following can be good for proving the credibility of your business, which is so important in these early stages.

I use Followliker for building my Twitter following. It's a social media tool that automates the following, unfollowing, direct messages, replies, favourites, and every other function imaginable.

This might not be to everyone's liking, you may prefer to build your following organically. But with this tool, I built my following to over 20,000 followers on many of our accounts, all for the one-time investment of $97.99 - it only takes one or two of those followers to proceed to buy from my business for that investment to pay-off.

The great thing when automating your following is that you can choose which accounts' followers and following to follow, which in-turn, a %age of those accounts will follow back and therefore become in-touch with what you are communicating. So, in the software you can input your closest competitors' Twitter accounts and it will scrape all of their followers, for you to then systematically and automatically follow. You can really finely-tune who you connect with using this tool by focusing on particular audiences.

The software itself has a great help guide should you choose to download it, so I won't get too much into the actual workings of it all here - but I will say it is an extremely effective piece of software and helps to rapidly build your Twitter following for credibility and also for direct sales.

I run Followliker on a VPS (Virtual Private Server) from Hostwinds, so it's running 24/7 and doesn't stop running its processes just because I've turned-off my computer.

Next, Facebook. Now, there are obvious methods to build a foundation of 'likes' for your Facebook page, sharing your page with friends for instance, or even running a paid advertising campaign on Facebook with the action of having someone like your page.

However, both of these things I have found to be relatively ineffective. The former only gets likes from people on the basis of your relationship with them, they aren't actually that interested in the product or service you're selling, and the latter don't often convert to customers - reason being, having someone like your page doesn't give you unrivaled access to share things with that person and for them to see it on their feed. Facebook don't allow too much communication with your following unless you're paying them to promote a particular message.

Now, the technique and software I'm about to tell you about is not for every business - I've personally steered away from using this tool for the vast majority of my businesses on moral grounds, but I do use it on a couple of blogs I own, and it does have a massive impact on your 'likes'.

The software is called 'LikeJacker' - it's a black hat software, that you install on your site and it's available from blackhatworld.com.

It sits on your site, and recognises whether or not a visitor is signed-in to their Facebook account. If they are, any click they make on your website, whether they are looking at a product, reading your terms, visiting a page, will result in them 'liking' your Facebook page.

It's stealthy, and rather underhand some might say. But my logic for allowing this on the blogs I own is that these people are already on your website, they are clearly interested in what you are offering, so having them like your Facebook page is not the worst thing in the World - you aren't forcing this on people who really aren't interested in what you're offering.

You have to be very careful about how many likes you permit per day - if Facebook find you are using tactics like this, they will ban your page. However, I personally managed to build around 2,000 likes on one blog's page in a few months without notice - so if you do it slowly, over time, you should be okay.

And those are the two techniques I have used to build my Facebook and Twitter followings in the past. There are other techniques, and of course you can take the completely organic route if you prefer, but if you want thousands of followers quickly, and you don't have hundreds of pounds to spend on social media promotion, then these techniques work perfectly.

Next up, I'll show you how to get the most out of PPC using Bing and Adwords ads effectively, so they deliver a positive Return on Investment.

DAY 15 - GOOGLE ADWORDS AND BING ADS: PAY AS LITTLE AS 1P PER CONVERSION USING PPC CLERVERLY

Pay-Per-Click can be a very expensive way to advertise your website and your products and services.

In some industries that my businesses operate, you can pay up to £10 per click just to get on the front page of Google results. That's insane!

You'd have to have enormous gross margins and an amazing conversion rate to make that cost-per-click profitable.

But, there are ways to use PPC that don't cost a fortune. It's a broad discipline, and takes a lot of different forms, and I'm about to show you which ones work the best for us in terms of minimising cost, and maximising Return on Investment.

Again, all of these techniques won't be applicable to all business models - it'll be up to you to decide which methods would suit your particular business and to implement accordingly.

I won't talk you through every micro-step of setting-up a campaign on Adwords and Bing Ads - Google and Microsoft employ people who can talk you through every single step on the telephone, and will probably provide more information on the features than I can.

What I will do, however, is highlight the 'type' of campaigns you should be exploring in order to maximise your Return on Investment - and you can communicate these to your account reps when you're going through the process of setting-up your campaigns - so they can show you exactly how to get these running for your site.

- Google Shopping

If your business isn't ecommerce, you can skip to the next technique here - Google Shopping is designed purely for websites selling physical products.

These are the results that show when you search for an item on Google, and it returns back the images with the item title and price shown in the actual search results. These listings are also accessible via the 'shopping' link on Google.

The great thing about them is their transparency - if yours is the cheapest offering for a particular item, then it's quite clear to people searching for the item that yours is the best deal, because your price is shown right at the side of your competitors' prices - even before they've clicked into your website.

Because of this transparency, and because they are geared towards people searching Google with the intention of buying something, you get much fewer irrelevant clicks and people just searching for information with no intention of buying.

Plus, if you have a vast catalogue, and offer items that are not widely available from other sellers, the competition will be sparse on certain items, and you can start with the lowest possible bid of 1p per click for your full catalogue then work up from there.

To establish a Google Shopping Campaign, you'll first need to establish your product feed - this tells Google what products you have available on your website, and other details such as price, image, title and so on. Your Google rep will be able to assist you with the feed setup in the Google Merchant Centre, and with linking this to your Adwords account - you just need to ensure the feed is provided from your Wordpress site.

You will need to install a plugin to quickly and easily develop your feed, I use one called 'TFM Google Product Feed' which is free, it has no limits to how many products you can include in your feed and just adds 3 simple fields to the bottom of your product pages for you to complete, so the product can go live on the feed. Just ensure these are completed each time you create a new product, and your products will all push through to the feed successfully.

Then all you need to do is set-up an account for, or log in to, Google Merchant Centre and provide the necessary details as to where your feed is hosted (this information is available from within the plugin settings and details). Then run through all the merchant feed default settings for shipping prices, product category and so on. Your Google account rep will be able to assist with this if you have any trouble, and they'll also help you to link your feed into your Adwords campaign - but it's simply a task of grabbing your merchant centre account number and entering this during the setup of your shopping campaign.

- Video Campaigns

I'm going to cover video in more detail in a later section of the book, but here I just want to highlight how effective a video campaign can be via Google Adwords.

So, production of the video aside, once you have some video content to share, upload them to Youtube, and you can start to promote these via your Adwords account to give them more visibility.

We've seen some great conversion rates from video campaigns in the past, and the CPC tends to be a lot lower than standard search campaigns. Always use a call-to-action overlay on your Youtube videos so people can click a link to visit your site and buy what you are advertising. But, again, more on video marketing in a later section of this book.

- Remarketing

From the moment you open your Adwords account, even if you don't set-up your campaigns right away, the first thing you should do is activate your audiences.

Go to 'Shared Library' and under this, select 'Audiences'. In here you'll see a red button called 'Remarketing Lists'. Hit this button, and from the dropdown select 'website visitors'.

You can segment your audiences as far as you like, creating separate audiences for people who convert on your website ie make a purchase, people who leave after visiting a particular page, and so on. But to be honest, unless you're developing separate banners and other materials to specifically target each segment, then just stick to one audience list - at least to begin with - the people who visit your website.

Now, if you don't already know, remarketing is basically a way of displaying targeted ads to people who have been on your site previously. Meaning you can build a stronger brand awareness amongst your existing customer base and prompt them to re-purchase, and you can build credibility with those that visited but didn't purchase, and maybe draw them back to make a purchase.

It's got much lower CPC compared to pushing adverts to cold prospects, and generally has a much better conversion rate - because the people you are marketing to are already familiar with your brand, they have been on your site before.

If your website is ecommerce, you can opt to run dynamic remarketing ads, which we have found to be particularly powerful, so in the advert it shows products on your site that the person has already been viewing, and similar items. So not only are you remarketing to familiar prospects, you're also remarketing familiar products from your site, ones they have an active interest in.

Again, tell your Google Adwords rep that you want to set remarketing up, and they'll guide you through the whole process.

- Brand-Focused Search Campaigns

This is something that works great perhaps when your brand has become a little more established.

We generally steer away from cold search campaigns - one, because Adwords offers better fits for our business models like Shopping and Video, and two, because it's generally the most expensive and crowded avenue of PPC.

But, if you have a brand recognised by people, then it's worth putting up a brand-based search campaign - so people actively searching for your company can find you easily.

And I'm not saying run search campaigns for products or services you re-sell, that have an established brand - that would be expensive and potentially very time-consuming to set-up and manage. I mean your brand, your website name, your company name. People who are actively looking to visit YOUR site, or buy YOUR products or services.

This is low-hanging fruit, it produces great conversion rates and a low CPC, and nothing stops your competitors jumping in on your brand keywords to steal these customers - so it's often just a good idea to run a campaign like this to give you visibility above the competition so your brand-followers can't be drawn away too easily.

- Bing Ads

When it comes to PPC, Google Adwords is by far the market leader. However, it pays not to completely dismiss the other platforms - for a small business, they do still have a sizable audience, and what's more, this platform is a lot, lot cheaper and less crowded than Google Adwords.

This means, you're targeting potentially the same people as you do via Google Adwords, with exactly the same value proposition, except for potentially 10x less cost per click. It becomes pretty obvious that this can become a very profitable way to market your products and services.

The only difference is, you won't generate AS MANY sales as you would through Adwords, because there's less of an audience, but the sales you do make will highly likely be much more profitable - so don't overlook this platform.

The great thing about Bing ads is that you can import your settings directly from Google Adwords, so it's quick and easy to get it all set-up and you don't need to spend time building your campaigns all over again on this separate platform.

So, that summarises my tips with regards to making the most of your PPC advertising.

On a final note, before you go ahead and sign-up for your Google Adwords or Bing Ads accounts and contact your account reps, remember the principles of bootstrapping your cashflow from last week?

Well, these are paid advertising platforms, so it's important to get as much from them as you can.

Log back into your Hostgator CPanel, and in there you will find access to some promotional vouchers for both of these platforms

- providing you with free clicks to get you started without incurring any initial costs, so you can check that the campaigns I've mentioned will work for your particular site before you commit financially.

If it doesn't work out after your free balance runs-out, and you haven't converted any customers, you can cancel your campaigns and move-on, and if it does work out and you've managed to convert some customers through these channels using your free trial balance, then great! You've just got some highly-profitable first customers for your business - keep it running, and keep tweaking your campaigns with the help of your account manager to make sure you are minimising your cost per conversion, and maximising your sales.

Make sure you speak to your account rep about setting up conversion tracking before you set your campaigns live, so you can make sure you understand what is working and what isn't for your campaigns.

Next up, I'll show you how to build a network of affiliate partners to extend your reach and boost your sales with an effectively commission-only salesforce.

DAY 16 - AFFILIATE PROGRAM: BUILD A SALES TEAM

An affiliate program allows you to build a network of salespeople that refer people to your site, in return for a payment when those referred people convert into customers.

It's one of the safest ways to market your start-up, given you don't have any fixed advertising costs - you only pay a %age or a fixed fee, whenever a sale is made. If no sales are made, you owe your affiliates nothing.

Get the right affiliates on-board, and it could be one of the most effective forms of advertising and traffic channels for your website.

Now, there's two options when it comes to developing an affiliate network. You can use a third-party managed service and platform like Commission Junction, which often involves a steep up-front cost, or you can use a self-hosted solution.

In all of our businesses, we use self-hosted affiliate programs.

On Wordpress, there's a great plugin called 'Affiliates Manager' that you can install and activate, and it will allow affiliates to register, get links, and manage their accounts online.

In terms of banners and materials, refer back to your Fiverr designer to get some made-up for next to nothing, so you can give your affiliates plenty of good-looking assets to promote your site and your products/services.

When you've installed this plugin, and your program is all set-up with banners uploaded and ready, you need to promote your affiliate program so you can start to build your network.

Start by contacting blogs and other information-based sites to see if they would be interested in joining your program and placing some banners on their site.

A great resource when searching for sites to partner with is buzzsumo.com.

On this site, you can enter some keywords related to your particular business or industry, and it will draw back all the articles related to your keywords and ranks them according to their social reach.

The ones that rank either have a great topic that's gone viral, or it shows that the site has some serious readership and social power - these are potentially very effective affiliates for your business.

Contact all the sites that return for keywords relevant to your website and products - and even if you only land one of these out of 100, then they are highly likely to bring some business your way.

You can only draw back a few top results without upgrading to Buzzsumo pro, and you can't filter according to Country etc on the free version either, but you should be able to think of plenty of keyword variations to search for so you can trawl all the top results and build a pretty long list of websites to contact and push your program to.

Once you've built a small network of affiliates from your outreaching, it's essential that you keep in-touch with them. Let them know when any new marketing materials are released or special offers/content gets posted to your site, so they can push this too, and ask them questions - make sure they have everything they need to push your ads effectively, and they are satisfied with the program, the last thing you want to do is lose them because they are dissatisfied in some way.

And that concludes how to establish and build an affiliate network for your business.

In the next section of the book, I'll show you how to develop and promote potentially viral videos to help push awareness and traffic for your site.

DAY 17 - VIDEO MARKETING: CREATE POTENTIALLY VIRAL VIDEO ADS AND PROMOTE FOR AS LITTLE AS 1P PER VIEW

If you've ever tried video marketing before, you might be thinking - I've created videos before, put them on Youtube and Vimeo, and they've only had a couple of hundred views.

Well, you wouldn't be alone in this - and I've seen this happen many times in the past with my own businesses, but not anymore.

As soon as you realise that platforms like Youtube and Vimeo - along with any other social media channel - aren't advertising platforms in themselves. These are crowded platforms, with plenty of other individuals and businesses (your competitors included) vying for people's attention.

As soon as you realise that each social media platform is like a little micro-business in its own right, where you have to strategise your content, and find ways to promote and push through the noise of others, then that's when you'll start to see success on these platforms.

Just like with a website, you can't just throw a video up and expect it to accumulate views - you have to find ways to build that initial momentum, that foundation of viewers that can then help spread viewership through social sharing and word of mouth.

Yes, your video may show for search results, but given how many videos are now on platforms like Youtube, it's near on impossible to find a niche subject that hasn't already been covered - and with a new video and profile, you'll struggle to push past the more established videos and profiles on the platform - meaning your video stays way down the search results, accumulating little to no views.

Even if your video is amazing, if you get stuck in this trap, noone will see it to be able to share it, so you never end-up building the momentum that your video needs to become visible.

Therefore, for a video to be successful, it needs 3 things:

1. Great content
2. Relevance and popularity/demand in your chosen niche
3. Initial momentum and foundation views

So, first of all, we need great content. We need to devise a clever video, based around popular keywords relative to our business - and this is what will keep the momentum going once you've established your foundation viewership.

Perhaps you can build an instructional video on how to solve a common problem your customers have - with the goal of building awareness and establishing yourself as having expertise in this particular field.

Or maybe your business has a particular cause or purpose that it wants to share, and you can think of funny, smart, and innovative ways to communicate this message on video - just like a commercial. Watch related adverts on Youtube to get some inspiration for the concept.

Whatever it may be, it needs to be engaging, and valuable to the viewer - they need to be motivated to watch for either the purpose of gaining knowledge to solve a problem they have, as with instructional videos, or it needs to be particularly entertaining or funny for them to watch, as with the commercial type videos.

Don't think just because you're interested in your business, that other people will be. Start your content creation process through the eyes of the viewer or the customer, what's in it for them? Is it entertainment value, for gaining knowledge, or some other benefit?

Noone is really interested that your were incorporated in 2016 or that you sell a range of plumbing supplies online. Your video HAS to be engaging - you can communicate more about your business and products to the people who click through your video call-to-action and visit your site to read more. This is the time to be creative, and valuable to the viewer.

Once you have your video concept, head over to Fiverr.com again, and choose a video producer, an actor, and/or a video editor - find whatever providers you need to make your video concept a reality, and choose who to work with.

Then upload your video to Youtube.

Having viewed the concept creation through the eyes of the viewer or customer, the video should already be relevant to them, but now you need to find the keywords to use in your video title and description to maximise the organic traffic your video will receive.

A great tool to use for this can be found in your Google Adwords account. Log into your Google Adwords dashboard and go to tools > display planner.

You'll then be faced with several fields and settings. Just change the ad formats and sizes part to 'video' only, and enter the keywords you are considering for your video.

This will then return back several alternative keyword suggestions in that area, and show you how popular each one is - so you can focus on the high-traffic keywords and give yourself the best chance of receiving maximum organic traffic on Youtube.

So now you have your video uploaded and titled, and ready for people to watch.

Here's where you need to build your initial momentum and viewership.

Now, I'm not saying this is the only way to do it, because it's not, but the best method (in terms of cost and conversion) that we have found for our businesses is to combine your Youtube video with Facebook ads.

On here, we pay as little as 1p per view, and therefore managed to accumulate over 2,000 views in 4 days for one of our videos, with an ad spend of just £20.

Share your Youtube video on your Facebook page, then visit the 'Adverts Manager' area on Facebook to boost your post, or click the blue 'boost post' button at the bottom of your page in the Pages Manager app.

This will allow you to design an ad campaign around your video post, and gain more exposure and views on the Youtube platform.

You can also promote your Youtube videos via Adwords itself like I explained in an earlier section of the book - so using these two methods combined, even for a short period of say 2-3 weeks, to limit your costs, should give you a good, solid foundation of views and therefore help with developing a foundation for social sharing, word of mouth, and visibility on Youtube itself.

And that summarises video advertising - you should now know everything you need to create engaging video content, and get it noticed - for very little investment.

Tomorrow, I'll show you how to branch out from your website platform and use other third-party platforms to effectively sell your products and services on. I'll tell you which ones are the best, and the easiest to use - so you can quickly and easily boost the growth of your business for very little risk and no additional investment except a little time.

DAY 18 - THIRD-PARTY PLATFORMS: GREAT PLATFORMS FOR PHYSICAL AND NON-PHYSICAL GOODS AND SERVICES

One quick, low-risk way of gaining customers is to sell your products or services on 3rd Party platforms, alongside your website.

These are generally established marketplaces that already have a customer-base and a familiar audience, and you only get charged a %age of what you sell, so if you make no money (generally) there aren't any fees to pay.

Depending on what you are selling, the following platforms may be worth exploring:

- Amazon

Amazon is the number 1 ecommerce platform. Millions of people shop on this platform every single day, and they sell everything from batteries, to fresh meat! So if you're selling physical products, you can probably bet you can sell them on Amazon.

Amazon show customers all offers from sellers, but they give the cheapest and best-value offerings what they call 'the buy box' - making this the most obvious choice for customers adding items to their basket.

What that means is, the platform can become fiercely competitive. A lot of sellers use auto-pricing software (now being offered by Amazon themselves) to undercut other sellers by 1p so they constantly own the buy-box, and this shuts out other sellers who aren't using this sort of software on their listings. Imagine trying to manually ensure you maintain the buy box on a catalogue of just 1,000 products, checking and adjusting prices each day - only to be undercut by a penny a couple of hours later and lose the buy-box.

Combined with fees of 15% and a monthly subscription cost for your account, plus demanding seller metrics, and the challenge of maintaining synchronised stock levels across your website and this platform, not to mention managing fulfillment from them both, it makes Amazon a very challenging prospect. BUT, there's still a huge opportunity if you have the right margins on your items, and you're properly geared-up for price wars with other sellers. Amazon gives you access to scale that can sometimes make-up for the lack of a generous margin on each item sold.

So, if you're going to explore this concept, you need to be prepared. There is software and plugins out there designed to make branching-out to this platform easier, synchronising stock levels, drawing back orders into the fulfillment area of your site so you can despatch all from one place, marking orders as shipped on the Amazon platform when you mark them as shipped on your website, and also access to auto-pricing tools.

Personally, I wouldn't entertain the idea of exploring the Amazon platform without using something like this - it's too low-margin, and too much manual work to be worthwhile. But if you have the right fulfillment infrastructure in-place to handle scale, and the right software installed, it can be a largely automated way to boost your revenue and earn a little more profit if done properly.

With Amazon, you will also have the ability to explore its International platforms - you can create listings on 4 European platforms through your UK account login, FR, DE, IT, and ES. If you want to sell to the US and Canadian markets, you'll need to set-up a separate account on amazon.com.

- Ebay

Ebay is a similar platform to Amazon, except a little less price-competitive. Ebay doesn't amalgamate seller listings so customers can see these all in one place, your listing will stand alone - so the pricing difference compared to the competition is less obvious.

Because of this, it can be a more profitable platform, combined with the fact that Ebay fees are generally around 5% less than Amazon.

That said, you do pay a small fee per listing to create them initially, so if you have a huge catalogue of slow-moving lines, it can become loss-making or simply wipe-out your profit, so you have to choose your lines carefully.

View completed listings for similar products, and see what they have sold for and how frequently they sell, so you get an idea for what will be worth listing on this platform or not.

The same principles apply to Ebay as they do to Amazon, you'll need a plugin or some other software to link to this platform to keep stock synchronised, prices synchronised, orders synchornised, and shipments centralised.

I would advise against exploring the Ebay platform without this in-place beforehand.

- Etsy

Similar to Ebay, but more for handmade arts and crafts.

It carries listing fees but these typically cover the listing for 4 months - but for each unit you sell, you'll effectively pay the listing fee again for the listing to remain live (regardless of how man units of stock you allocate at the outset). Selling fees are much lower than the other two platforms discussed, at just 5% of the sale value of each item.

Again, the same principles apply, look for a reliable plugin or software that you can centralise everything with if you're going to explore this channel.

Those are the 3 main third-party platforms for physical goods, but there's also others you could explore like newegg.com and others.

In terms of digital products like books and ebooks, there's some great platforms like Udemy, eHow, Warrior Forum, Warrior Plus, JVZoo, and many more.

You can use a third-party platform to sell all your digital items through, and just redirect your site to the enrollment, sign-up, or checkout process on these platforms, or if you want to maximise your profitability, you may want to sell direct on your site alongside these other platforms, as they all obviously take their respective share of your income - in some cases up to 75%.

In terms of services, such as consulting, professional services, creative and design services and so on, then you may wish to explore Fiverr.com (as a provider this time), Upwork, PeopleperHour, Toptal, or Freelancer.co.uk.

Although very different in their audience and focus, the high-level concept of these sites are the same, they allow someone to offer their services on a freelance basis for money.

Whether it's a case of trawling and bidding on 'tenders' like on

Upwork, so you take a pro-active approach to the projects you work or bid on, or whether it's a case of building a gig on Fiverr and putting it out there for people to order, it's worth exploring these platforms if you're just getting started as a freelance service provider - it can be a quick and easy way to develop a foundation of clients.

Back when I started my copywriting agency whilst I was studying Business at University, I used Elance (which became Elance-Odesk, and is now known as Upwork) to bid on projects that people wanted completing. It wasn't high-paid work, because we had no portfolio, and we were bidding against other providers in a competitive, transparent environment, but it developed our foundation of clients, and our portfolio, that we were then able to grow from.

So that wraps-up this section of the book, and I hope some of the platforms I've mentioned here will be relevant to your business and allow you to promote and grow your business rapidly from the outset.

Tomorrow, I'll show you how to make the most of your organic search engine traffic through some simple Search Engine Optimisation techniques.

DAY 19 - SEO: MAXIMISE THE FREE TRAFFIC YOUR SITE RECEIVES

Now, I'm going to be honest - I'm not that into SEO.

There are a ton of so-called SEO experts out there that advocate or conduct black-hat techniques such as link farming, keyword spamming, and so on.

What normally happens, when you try to play the algorithms of a super-smart tech giant like Google, and don't play precisely by their rules, you get penalised or even worse, wiped from search results completely.

Google hold an enormous amount of power over online businesses, they can wipe you off the radar if they wanted to - so don't break their rules!

The thing about organic search results is, they're organic. They shouldn't be forced or controlled by advertising spend or manipulative techniques employed by SEO experts. They are, quite rightly, controlled by user experience and value. If Google believes your site is valuable for users searching for a particular subject, they'll rank you for it.

All SEO is about, therefore, in my mind, is following Google's tips on how to make your site crawler-friendly and keyword-rich, and gaining genuine, valuable, and relevant backlinks to help bolster your credibility through the eyes of Google.

Nothing too complicated, nothing too spammy or manipulative.

That's why I'm not that into it - there's nothing to get 'into'. The underlying mantra is simple, provide valuable, unique content for visitors.

Google employ some of the smartest minds in the World. If you think you can manipulate their algorithms by outsmarting the people that create and tweak them for a living, then good luck. But I won't be teaching you how to do that, I'm not smart (or, perhaps, stupid) enough.

So, my guide to SEO is simple and comprises of two parts:

1. On-site optimisation following Google's own advice
2. Build genuine, relevant backlinks for credibility

That's it!

So, starting with part 1, you're already in an advantageous position by having built your website on Wordpress - which is already SEO optimised to a large extent, and provided your chosen theme is a responsive design to mobile, then you'll be ticking one of the most important boxes for Google.

To tick as many other boxes as you can, search 'Google Webmaster Guidelines', find the guide hosted on support.google.com and work down the tips provided by Google themselves - after all, they're the ones you're trying to impress, why listen to anyone else?

Then, once you've made sure that you are satisfying Google's own on-site requirements, move onto part 2.

There are two techniques I use for building credible, valuable, and relevant backlinks - one is to build and distribute press releases to relevant news sites whenever my businesses have something newsworthy to shout about. If you get published in a major news site like the BBC, Guardian, or The Times, this will give your site more credibility in Google's eyes than 1,000 links from low pagerank sites.

The second technique is to seek out relevant sites that would benefit their visitors if they were to link to your site in some way - for instance if your product or service is complimentary to their offering, or if you're a reseller for a particular brand, then contact them to see if they can list you on their 'where to buy' page or something similar.

Always view initiated link-building from a perspective of visitor value, and as though search engines don't exist. If your link on someone else's site isn't going to provide genuine value to someone visiting that site, then it shouldn't be on there.

Forcing too many backlinks on irrelevant sites looks suspicious, and will not help your rankings. Keep it genuine, and focus on visitor value - then your goals are always aligned with Google's own goals, and you can't go far wrong.

SEO takes time. You can't build genuine, valuable links at a rate of hundreds per day, and even things like the age of your domain are said to impact your strength in rankings. So be patient, and stay on the right side of the rules, with your goals strictly aligned with those of Google. It will pay-off in the long-run.

Tomorrow, I'll show you how to use email marketing effectively in order to maximise visitor value and encourage conversions.

DAY 20 - EMAIL: REMARKET TO EMAIL LEADS AND PREVIOUS CUSTOMERS COST-EFFECTIVELY

Email is one of the most cost-effective forms of advertising and remarketing to existing customers.

In fact, with Mailchimp, your first 2,000 subscribers, or 12,000 emails per month, are completely free.

You should have already set-up a Mailchimp account and set-up your lead capture form via the Mailchimp for Wordpress plugin that I mentioned in an earlier section of the book.

You can also incorporate a tick-box or something similar during the checkout process so that all people purchasing from your site can opt-in to your email list.

Once your list has started to accumulate, then it's time to start running campaigns to your list to try to get those people to either convert or buy more from you.

You might want to advertise new product or service launches, special discounts, or new website features to your list.

The general rule is to view your emails from a reader's perspective. If you think the reader will find value in what you are saying, then tell them. If they won't, then don't send the email.

If you send too many irrelevant or valueless emails, you'll get a high unsubscribe rate and lose your audience - so don't send emails out for the sake of sending emails, make sure they deliver value.

If you're running a special promotion to your list, always make it time-limited, to encourage action there and then. With most of our retail businesses we run 24-hour only promotions - these force the subscriber to decide whether they want to purchase the offer there and then, or not. They can't say to themselves that the offer will be around next week, and they'll buy then.

In terms of design and layout, Mailchimp do offer quite a few free templates that you might want to use initially, but Fiverr.com is another great resource here. You can get a newsletter template design made-up for $5, that you can just amend slightly each time you send a mailer.

And finally, analyse your reports and test. Each time you send a mailer you'll be able to draw-back all sorts of data like open rates and click-through.

Always make sure you analyse the results of these before you send your next mailer, so you can get an idea for what sort of headlines encourage good open rates, and what offers encourage people to click through to your site from the email - these metrics will allow you to understand your market, and what they find true value in, so you can build even more relevant and effective content going forward.

You may also wish to start splitting your lists depending on whether or not they have purchased from you before, or according to particular demographics or characteristics - which will allow you to finely tune their needs and drill-down further into what content each group finds valuable. You can also split-test your campaigns to see which ones work best. These techniques are a little more advanced though and perhaps better left to when you have established a strong subscriber list first.

And that concludes the third week of your book.

You should now have some good ideas for your promotional activity and be able to start gaining your first customers for next-to-no investment using the techniques I've taught you.

Once you've got your first few customers, you'll just need to scale-up your promotional activity focusing on what works for your business, and reinvesting in these particular techniques to win even more custom, alongside using remarketing to maximise customer order frequency.

At this point, your business is off the ground and trading - congratulations!

But the work doesn't stop there. In order to maintain what you have already built and to grow it further, you need to prepare to delegate where necessary, to automate processes wherever you can, to diversify your revenue streams and protect your business, to maximise customer order values through cross-selling and up-selling, to reinvest in your business, and to potentially find further funding to fuel growth.

There's lots of work, and fun, ahead! In next week's chapters, the final week of your 4-week book, I'm going to show you how you can implement all of these things to ensure the consistent growth of your business.

DAY 21 - THE ART OF DELEGATION: WHEN AND HOW TO DELEGATE TASKS SO YOU CAN FOCUS ON GROWTH

Your journey in business so far has seen you do mostly everything yourself - with the exception of involving an accountant and outsourcing certain requirements like design.

But going forward, as you grow, you'll need to learn to delegate responsibility and control of your business to other people.

Your time is a finite resource.

If you don't learn how to delegate, pretty soon you'll find you're expending all of your time simply maintaining your business and running day-to-day activities. The only way to break through this glass-ceiling, and win more time to grow your business, is to bring other people in.

I've been through the transition of bootstrapping a start-up and being involved in every micro-process, to delegating pretty much everything involved in running the business day-to-day, many times over.

It's a difficult transition to make, and it's made even more difficult if you don't find the right people to delegate to, and put people in the right place within your business.

In my view, there are 3 levels of personal growth you have to go through as your business grows, in order to delegate effectively:

1. As your start-up grows, you need to be bold. You need to entrust people with responsibility to take-over the roles you once played, and accept that they may play these roles slightly differently to the way you did, and they may make some mistakes (especially early on).

For me, this is the hardest stage of personal development regarding delegation. When you're engrossed in the micro-processes of your business, it's easy to remain here, thinking noone can perform your particular roles better than you do, or thinking you can do it yourself and save cash. It's a trap to think this way, and stunts the growth of your business severely.

It's hard to get out of this mindset, and there's no other way of breaking free from this thought process than to literally throw yourself out of it and hand over the responsibility to someone else when finances permit, and when you feel you don't have enough time to work ON the business, rather than working IN the business.

To go far, you need other people behind you.

Don't be afraid to hand this responsibility over. Just be certain that you have the right person for the role, in terms of their core strengths and weaknesses.

When you bring people on-board, you'll go through the necessary application and interview process, where you can make theoretical and gut-feeling decisions about who's right for your advertised role.

But, it's only when they're in the business, and you see how their strengths and weaknesses play out in practicality, that you can truly decide who is suited to a particular role.

As a small business, bringing people in, you will highly likely be wanting your employees to conduct several roles in the business - you won't be big enough to offer dedicated roles in particular niche fields of your business, like Google Adwords management, or customer service, or whatever. You will highly likely be offering applicants a role that involves wearing many hats.

So, use this to your advantage.

Assess how employees perform in each role, decide where you think their true motivations and strengths lie, and use this feedback to form a perfectly-suited role for each employee - based on what they are good at, and what they truly enjoy. And this morphs into step 2 of personal development when it comes to delegation:

2. Understand and appreciate that employees aren't as interested in your business as you are.

They just don't have the same investment - both emotional and financial - as you do in your business. Unless they possess an insane work ethic, they probably won't be staying behind to finish things until 10pm each night, then coming back in at 6am the following morning - generally speaking, only entrepreneurs working on their own businesses are really this driven over the long-term.

So, just as you did when you decided on the concept of your business - found your passion to ensure you remain motivated around growing it and making it successful, you need to adopt this same consideration for your employees.

They have their own passions, their own interests, their own motivations, and their own objectives - and it's up to you as their leader to ensure their role remains engaging and motivating for them. Otherwise, you'll either lose them, or you'll see productivity take a nose-dive over time as interest wanes.

So listen to them, and understand that it's not just your business needs that are important when fulfiling a role, you also need to appreciate the needs of the employee, and find a balanced situation where both of these sets of needs are being satisfied through effective allocation of roles to the right people.

Felix Dennis once said that the only skill you need as a business owner is to learn how to find and retain talent - and you'll reach success.

And a way to retain talent once you've found it, is to ensure your talent remains motivated and engaged by what they do.

Then onto step 3 of personal development regarding delegation - and if you reach this stage, then you know you're doing something right, because your business will be sizable at this point:

3. Find someone that appreciates and understands the first 2 steps, and put them in charge of HR. So you can unlearn steps 1 and 2, and continue to be an entrepreneur, not a business manager.

At this point, you're learning how to delegate to delegators. You're handing over the recruitment and human resource management to someone else - which, in my mind, is THE most important, crucial, and significant step in a growing business.

Get this wrong, and the first 2 principles will be undermined. Everything you have built to this point will slowly unravel as employees lose interest and engagement because they aren't being monitored and moulded into the right roles.

The employment of your first HR manager is critical. Take the importance of steps 1 and 2, and amplify this by 1000.

You need to find a HR manager that has a true connection and understanding of people, and who is motivated by these connections and helping people thrive in your business, and in-turn this will allow the business to thrive.

You need to find someone who is motivated by motivating people, you're matching a role to someone with the right strengths, who has the ability to match other roles according to strengths of other employees.

To me, your HR manager is your keystone to the business. They have to fit right. If they don't, your business will unravel.

And that's the art of delegation!

With this only being your 4th week in business, you'll still be quite a way off preparing for step 3, and perhaps even quite a way from steps 1 and 2 - your focus will initially be around gaining enough financial stability to be able to employ someone.

But, it's always good to be mindful of these steps before you reach them - so you can prepare in advance for them, and be conscious of what's required from you to grow your business.

Tomorrow, I'll teach you the art of automation - something you should have already adopted to varying degrees if you followed some of my advice from week 3 of this book, with the Twitter management software and so on - but I'm going to show you how automation can be used to grow your business AND save time and money in the process.

DAY 22 - THE ART OF AUTOMATION: IDENTIFY WHERE YOU CAN APPLY AUTOMATION IN YOUR BUSINESS TO SAVE TIME

I'm a huge fan of business automation - so much so I once started a blog called businessautomationtips.com, that I sold to Zynk (a software development firm specialising in Sage process automation) some years ago.

So, why is automating your business processes where possible so important?

Well, time costs money, if you or your staff are spending excessive amounts of time completing repetitive processes in your business, then you're missing out on the opportunity to allocate that time to something more important.

If you can automate most of your repetitive processes using free or low-cost software, or techniques, then you've just reduced the cost of that particular process by removing the labour aspect.

Repetitive processes are not value-adding processes - they can't be. You're doing the same thing day-in, day-out - there's no possible way it can be adding additional value to your business. All it's doing is sustaining a particular part of your business.

If you can automate the repetitive, non-value adding processes in your business, your time can be allocated purely to value-adding processes, which will enable rapid growth.

If you don't automate your repetitive processes, you get trapped sustaining your business, not making any real progress, and having your time sapped away by these daily activities.

Now, there's plenty of different forms of automation - I even touched on some techniques to automate your marketing and promotion in week 3 of this book - but the underlying principles of automating processes remains the same, start by seeking-out and pin-pointing the repetitive processes you follow every day.

Then, once you've listed your repetitive daily processes, you need to look at ways you can remove this from your daily to-do list.

In the last section I spoke about employing staff and delegating tasks to them - but truly repetitive, daily processes, should really be automated where possible - delegating repetitive daily tasks to staff does not solve the misdirection they bring to your business in regards to consistent growth. Just like you, staff should also be allocated to value-adding processes, and their focus on repetitive daily tasks should be absolutely minimised.

So, when you've created your list of repetitive daily tasks for yourself, do the same for each of your staff members (if you have any at this point), so you can see where their time is being spent, and where opportunities for automation exist.

One prime example of simple automation, that saved my staff

literally hours each week, was to introduce something we call a bulk print function for our Vitalife Health business.

Each day fulfillment staff were individually printing packing slips for every single order, and then going back to the list of orders once they had packed and sent the goods, to mark the orders as shipped, one-by-one.

Until I introduced a bulk print button at the top of the page. It cost around £70 for my developers to introduce this for me, and probably paid for itself in less than a week.

Now, they just hit the bulk print button in a morning, which automatically runs off all packing lists for pending orders, directing these straight to a laser printer, so they are ready to be picked from in just a matter of seconds.

What's more, hitting the bulk print button also marks these orders as shipped, so once the button is pressed, there's nothing more for fulfillment staff to do than to pick and pack the orders.

Over the past year or so, this has saved us thousands of pounds in staff time - and it was one of the simplest forms of automation I've ever introduced to one of our businesses.

So, this just proves, automation doesn't have to be complex - you just have to sit and think about how time can be saved on each process, and then find someone to implement the necessary software or website alterations for you. Again, Fiverr is a great resource for this, or Toptal for more advanced requirements.

Here's my top tips for finding automation solutions for your repetitive tasks:

Just note, I've kept these quite broad and high-level so that their application can be visualised in a range of situations and processes, and aren't specific to just one type of business or process.

1. Look for where you can introduce mass actions. Like the ex-

ample I provided, is there a way for you to combine several multiple, identical tasks, into one action that deals with them all.

2. Can software or other technology actually conduct the process in its entirety? A good example of this is using autoresponders for certain email communications - Woocommerce and other ecommerce platforms have these built-in as standard for order notifications, but service-sellers, or bloggers may want to set an autoresponder up to confirm delivery of work or the posting of new content to their site.

3. Can you lean more on your suppliers or customers to cover certain processes themselves, to remove or reduce the burden in-house? Self-serve checkouts at supermarkets are the perfect example of this type of automation, but for online business this could mean, if you have a blog you could invite guest posts from other writers to develop some content without your actual input, or if you have an ecommerce site, you could open up the platform like Amazon do, to allow brand-owners and other retailers to list their own products, and so on.

4. Use APIs or other automated connections to suppliers. This is more applicable to ecommerce than anything else, where you can hook-up APIs to courier systems so shipping paperwork can print upon processing of the orders, and also to supplier's catalogues so you can synchronise with their stock levels and offer a vast catalogue without actually holding the stock yourself, and perhaps even establish a dropship arrangement so you can outsource some or all fulfillment needs

5. Do you really need to conduct these processes at all? Sometimes, it's as simple as understanding whether the process taking up time is actually necessary for your business. Is it something you can remove completely by simplifying processes and removing unnecessary manual data entry? After all, there's no point in storing data unless it's actually being used.

I hope these tips will help you to analyse and identify areas where automation can take place, and also to understand how you could introduce automation to these particular processes.

Tomorrow, I'll show you how to identify other potential revenue streams for your business, so you don't have all your eggs in one basket, and you can start to spread the risk in your business and find other avenues for growth.

DAY 23 - DIVERSIFY: HOW TO IDENTIFY OTHER EASY REVENUE STREAMS TO DIVERSIFY AND PROTECT YOUR BUSINESS

What established, successful business do you know that just relies purely on one revenue stream?

You may be surprised to discover just how many revenue streams successful companies have when you delve a little deeper - monetising parts of their business you weren't even aware of.

And why do they do this?

Two reasons. To encourage further growth, and to protect their business.

Take this scenario:

You build a blog around a hot new topic, cassette players (yes, I've set this example in the 1960s - before the internet - so it's an impossible situation, but you'll get the point).

You establish yourself as the go-to resource for reviewing cassette players, you have a strong affiliate income from the players you recommend, and you've got yourself an office and some staff to help with running the business.

You're doing well.

Then suddenly, CD players launch, and noone wants a cassette player anymore. Traffic takes a nosedive, and so does your affiliate income.

At this point, you have overheads and financial commitments in your business, so you're forced with either diversifying to begin reviewing CD players to pick traffic back-up and boost your affiliate income back to the good-old cassette days, or your business dies.

This is an extreme example of reactive diversification - but it highlights the risks you face if you remain overly focused on just one revenue channel for your business.

You're exposed to environmental and economic changes that you can't control - and the only way to protect against these sort of changes is to diversify, so the impact of them is minimised.

If the cassette player blogger took part in some pro-active diversification before the introduction of CD players, and launched separate blogs around the subject of other things popular in that era like afros, bellbottoms, and lava lamps, then the nosedive on the cassette player blog would have been less devastating because they'd still have income from their other blogs whilst they altered the direction of their cassette player blog and adjusted to the market.

So, how can we identify areas of revenue diversification in our business?

Well, it's good to start by understanding the TYPE of diversification that you can adopt. There's an academic business model called Ansoff's Matrix - and this highlights the 4 main ways that a business can grow.

Ultimately, there's 4 categories:

- Launching a new product in a new market
- Launching an existing product in a new market
- Launching a new product in an existing market
- Selling more of an existing product in an existing market

The latter of these doesn't qualify as diversification, so we'll ignore this. But the other 3 are examples of what you can do to diversify your revenue streams.

It's often best to explore the new product in an existing market or existing product in a new market approach - the new product in a new market option is the highest-risk avenue, and often doesn't allow you to play on the strengths and infrastructure you've already built for your core business.

So, let's look at each of these two options in-turn.

Launching an existing product in a new market

This could mean International expansion, or focusing your advertising and promotion on different market segments that you haven't targeted previously.

By diversifying your markets, you limit the risk of localised environmental factors and trends impacting your business.

Launching a new product in an existing market

So, for this approach you can explore new products and services you could sell alongside your core offering, complimentary rather than competing products work well so you have the opportunity to cross-market them as 'add-ons' to the customer's initial purchase.

New products and services can extend as far as an ecommerce platform introducing paid advertising spots for suppliers to purchase banners to push sales of their lines on their platform, or subscription packages for products - not just necessarily extending your product or service range. Think broader, and as diverse as possible.

If you have a blog, you could charge guest bloggers to write articles and include a link to their site alongside your advertising income, or introduce affiliate links for products or services you recommend in your posts, and so on.

If you're selling an online book, you could also offer affiliate links for software that you recommend, or launch off-shoots from your original book for people to enroll and learn even more about a particular subject.

There's plenty of ways to diversify - from the extreme diversification of the Virgin brand spanning across industries from airlines to music, to the more subtle (and realistic, at this stage) diversification of a group of niche blogs, all selling diverse advertising options.

And that covers diversification for your business. Spend today thinking of potential avenues for diversification.

You're only in your 4th week of business, so it's not necessary to diversify right now, and would probably be quite damaging - you don't want to spread yourself too thin too quickly. There's a balance to be achieved between focus and diversification.

Just store these ideas somewhere, so when the time comes, you have avenues that you can explore to protect and grow your business further.

GAVIN EDLEY

Tomorrow, I'll show you a technique to supercharge your growth by focusing on increasing your customer order value using some simple techniques.

DAY 24 - INCREASE ORDER VALUE: HOW TO USE CROSS-SELLING, UP-SELLING, AND DOWN-SELLING TO MAXIMISE CUSTOMER VALUE

If you've ever been through the Vista Print or Go Daddy checkout processes, you'll witness the extremes of cross-selling, up-selling, and down-selling.

For me, there's a balance between being pushy and subtly suggesting other items to add to your order, and some companies do cross over into the pushy category.

But whether you're pushy with them or not, cross-selling, up-selling, and down-selling techniques work. They help increase customer order value and/or capture a customer that would otherwise leave your site because your core offering doesn't suit them for one reason or another.

For an ecommerce site, cross-selling works well when you have a broad catalogue of products, and especially when you capture data on your customers so you know which products and services to recommend that will likely convert with each particular customer - this is something Amazon are particularly good at.

It could take the form of a product carousel that appears when an item is added to cart, to suggest similar goods, it could be a 'similar products' range shown on product pages or throughout the checkout process, or it could be emailing new deals based on previous customer purchases.

For an information product or virtual course, it could mean a carefully defined sales funnel, whereby those that don't convert are channeled towards a smaller, cheaper product or short-course, and those that do convert are then offered a more advanced product or course - these are both good examples of down-selling and up-selling in this type of business.

Ultimately, the underlying principle remains the same - selling more to existing customers is a more profitable promotional and growth technique than seeking brand new customers and visitors to your site. So don't neglect this, and make sure you are getting maximum value from each customer every time they complete a transaction with you.

If someone decides to commit and make a purchase for a product or service on your site, it's much easier for them, at this point, to throw some other complimentary items in their cart that they would otherwise not buy in standalone format.

If you're selling sunglasses on your website, make sure you've also got a range of cases to offer customers, glasses wipes, and lens protectors for cross-sales, make sure you have a transitions option and high-end branded alternatives as up-sells, or cheap-and-cheerful options as downsells, maybe presented in an exit pop-up before the visitor leaves the site - you could even sell this at break-even level and use cross-sells to make these low-value down-sells profitable again.

There's endless techniques you can employ on your site, and tons of relevant plugins you can use to implement these techniques, once you have the products or services available for sale.

Ultimately, when you look at your Return on Investment for paid advertising like Google Adwords, the bigger the order value per conversion, the better the ROI, and the more conversions (regardless of order value) then inevitably the better the overall ROI on your campaigns - which is what cross-selling, up-selling, and down-selling techniques help to deliver.

Spend today searching for relevant plugins and implementing these techniques on your site, or planning the expansion in your offering so that you can start to introduce these techniques when you have broadened your range sufficiently.

Tomorrow, I'll cover where to focus your reinvestment efforts for maximum growth.

DAY 25 - REINVEST: WHERE TO REINVEST IN YOUR BUSINESS FOR MAXIMUM GROWTH

When your business is up-and-running, it can be tempting to take from it what you can on a personal level - you might see this as the reward for the effort you put-in setting it up.

But if you want to achieve real, consistent growth in your company, you have to reinvest what you can.

I've always reinvested in my businesses to the absolute maximum - paying myself a very small wage, and putting every penny into more growth projects for the business.

If you pay yourself a generous wage too soon, you'll sap the company of its available funds, leave it with not enough cash to reinvest, and eventually, the business will suffer - the infrastructure will deteriorate, you'll miss expansion opportunities, and your business will either gradually shrink or remain static.

The only way to achieve growth is to reinvest, and often that means at the expense of short-term returns for the business owner. Focus on reinvestment in the short and medium term, and in the long-term, you'll hopefully reach a point where you can reward yourself generously and still have enough cash in the business to reinvest and grow.

But where should you allocate your surplus financial resources to achieve maximum growth and return?

This, again, varies wildly depending on your business model. For the blogger, this could mean purchasing other domains and building new blogs to diversify their offering, for ecommerce, this may mean expanding their range and investing in further stock, or for virtual products, it may mean investing in improving your product, paying for proofreading, adding new sections, and so on.

But, as a general rule, there are 3 core areas for any business to focus its reinvestment.

Product/Service - so, reinvesting in product/service improvements, range diversification and growth

Infrastructure - so, your website, your business processes (fulfillment, recording equipment, computers, other machinery)

Marketing/Promotion - where else can you invest surplus cash in order to boost sales further and for a good ROI

Spend today thinking about where, within these 3 core areas, you should allocate any profit for reinvestment.

Your priorities for reinvestment in each of these three areas will depend on your type of business as I said earlier, but also on the stage of your business - you will need to focus your reinvestment on certain areas at certain times.

Without understanding your precise business model, I can't offer exact recommendations, but what I can do is give you a timeline of where we focused our reinvestment in one of our fastest-growing online retail businesses, so you can see what I mean about timing of reinvestment in certain areas.

So, I'm going to break it down into 3 stages of growth, start-up, growth, and maturity.

In the start-up phase, our focus for reinvestment was on the product range - we had to buy more stock, which in-turn allowed us to increase customer order values from an average of around £30 to an average of around £50. We also focused our reinvestment on our website - streamlining backend fulfillment processes to make these as efficient and low-cost as possible, and also introducing new features on the front-end to encourage repeat orders (through subscription packages), cross-selling (through product recommendations), customer retention (through abandon cart emails), and to improve conversion rate through various tweaks using our analytics data.

Then, in the growth phase, we purchased our own warehouse facility, so we could continue our expansion and improve fulfillment processes further. We also commissioned an advanced stock management project which aimed to send data back to us in real-time and remove the labour requirement from stock counting, alongside an app for staff to use to book new stock arrivals in and so on.

Then, when we reached maturity, when we had a broad range of stock and a robust website and business infrastructure, we focused our reinvestment on marketing and promotion, finding new ways to increase market share and awareness through unexplored channels of promotion. Alongside continual reinvestment and improvement of our website and infrastructure.

Now, as I said, your journey of reinvestment will differ according to your business model - but this is a great example of where to focus your efforts if your business is ecommerce, or similar.

Now, on paper, the process of reinvestment I've described sounds quite linear and simple - we accumulated cash, then piled that back into our business. But it doesn't often work like that, and sometimes you need to make reinvestments, even before your finances are ready to reinvest.

We used a mixture of debt and grant funding throughout this particular business's journey in order to achieve what we did with it.

That's why tomorrow, I'm going to show you where to look if you need funding for your business to fuel its growth, and how to maximise your chances of winning this funding.

DAY 26 - FUNDING: HOW TO FIND AND ACHIEVE SUITABLE FUNDING TO TAKE YOUR BUSINESS TO THE NEXT LEVEL

If you want your business to grow fast, you're probably, at some point during its growth, going to need funding.

Funding largely comes in 3 different forms: debt-based, equity-based, or grant funding

I've been through all 3 of these funding processes before at one point or another, and I'm going to go through each one in-turn, advising the best platforms for attaining each type, and how to maximise your chances of winning funding through these platforms.

1. Debt-based funding

This consists of loans and mortgages - where you borrow a fixed amount, with a set level of interest, and you repay over a fixed period of time.

The first point of call should, of book, be your bank. You can apply for either an overdraft facility (if you need to drawdown on the balance over a period of time), or a loan facility (if you need all of the funds available for a set date).

Now, your bank are best-positioned to decide whether to lend to you or not - they see what goes in and out of your account on a regular basis, and will be able to assess your affordability on the loan from this.

If you don't have any luck with the bank, then try Funding Circle at fundingcircle.com

They have a super-quick and easy process of approval. Just apply online, and send them your accounts, and they'll send this off to the underwriters for approval.

If you're approved by the underwriters, then that is great news, because the success rate of attaining funding on the platform after this stage is really high.

Once approved, your loan application will go live to their platform where you'll receive investment either from a collective of individual investors or one institutional investor. It's best to let the application run its book, even when you have achieved your funding goal, as it will reduce the interest rate as more competitive offers on interest come in.

You must be turning over at least £50,000pa and have filed accounts for a minimum of 2 years to use Funding Circle.

We've used them numerous times, and they have been a great resource in allowing us to grow our businesses.

There's other platforms similar to Funding Circle like Funding Tree and many others, if you'd like to explore these instead.

The criteria for attaining debt-funding differs from platform to platform and from bank to bank, so don't be too disheartened if you're refused funding from one source. Keep searching and making applications elsewhere.

To increase your chances of attaining debt funding, it is a good idea to only explore this after a good couple of years of profitable trading. If you don't have this behind you, then you may need to skip to the other 2 funding options instead.

2. Equity-based funding

Attaining equity-based funding may be a better option if you aren't yet established enough to attain debt-based funding.

However, the process of attaining equity-based funding isn't quite as easy or straightforward in my experience.

Even on established equity-based crowd-funding platforms like Crowdcube that make it seem like a structured, step-by-step process of setting up your pitch and winning investment, you need external support and commitment from backers even before your campaign goes live here if you want to reach your investment target.

You can start by researching and building a list of angel investors in your particular field, and contacting them to see if they are willing to meet to discuss the proposition (be prepared to meet investors face-to-face, rarely do professional angel investors make large investments without first meeting the owners of the start-up at least once).

Check out angel.co and list your pitch and business here, then start contacting potential investors on this platform to build some initial interest.

Crowd-funding platforms, in my opinion, and from experience, shouldn't be used as stand-alone fundraising tools - they rarely work like this. What they are good for, is amplifying and topping-up the funds committed by one or several angel investors. I wouldn't list on a crowdfunding equity platform without first attaining at least 50% of your required funds from sources external to the platform beforehand.

These initial funds might be from professional investors, or they may even be from friends and family.

Venture Capitalists only tend to get involved with businesses once they are more established, so I wouldn't waste much time with these until you've been trading a good number of years, and your accounts show good growth - focus on angel investors if your business is still early-stage when you start to seek investment.

Attaining equity-based funding successfully is very heavily weighted on your own personal experience in business and/or your team's experience. If you can show a solid track record amongst your team, in a similar field to that in which your business operates, then you'll have ticked one of the biggest boxes for investors.

If you follow the earlier principles of reinvesting in your business and paying yourself very little, this will also look good to investors who want to see that you are serious about growing the business, and not too focused on your own personal needs, so that they are likely to see a strong return in 3-5 years time.

You'll also need an exit plan for your business before you go down the equity-funding route. This may seem crazy at such an early stage in starting your business, but investors won't invest in something without an end-goal. They need to know roughly when and how they'll see their return on their investment. Think about who you could sell to, or if you could list on the public market by around 3-5 years from now, and how much your business will be worth by then based on your projections.

One final consideration regarding applying for equity-based funding is how you value your business. Now, this isn't an exact science and valuations differ wildly. In the past I've valued businesses on the basis of 4x profit figure plus asset value - which seems to be a pretty standard method of valuing most trading businesses. However depending on your model, you may want to choose a different valuation method that aligns properly with your business.

3. Grant funding

For me, this is the most preferable form of funding - because you ultimately don't have to pay it back.

Of course, most grants come with commitments, where you have to employ x number of people or achieve certain targets for the grant to not become repayable, but provided you meet these, grant funding can be free money.

We've used several forms of grant funding across our businesses through the years, from localised retail funding for shop-fitting costs and local marketing activities, to website development grants, to grants to make property purchases.

I'm not going to lie, the application process can be quite long-winded and drawn-out, and you often have to get 3 sets of quotes for every cost aspect of the project (which, to be honest, is prudent anyway, regardless of who's money you're using). But if you can achieve the grant award at the end of it all, then it can be a hugely rewarding process and a way to add immediate value to your business, with no debt to negate this extra value.

The best place to start is by doing some local grant searches. Contact your local business support agency within the Council (most, if not all, Councils have them), and see if they can perform a local grant funding search for you, so you can assess which ones will be suitable for you to make applications for.

Then broaden your reach and do some national, or even International, grant searches. Projects that involve a good degree of research and development in particular fields can attract grant funding from specialised organisations and groups.

Never pay for someone to search for grant funding for you. Google is the best platform for this, just make sure you use keywords that ensure only relevant grant funds return back - such as ones in your local area, your industry, or your type of business.

Then get applying and see what happens! You've nothing to lose except a little time, and a lot to gain.

And that concludes this section of your book. Hopefully this gives you some ideas as to where you can go to apply for further funding should you need it down the line, and to help you prepare for applying for funding across the 3 different types discussed.

Tomorrow will be the final day of your 4-week book, where I'll be saying farewell and giving you some final pointers to take with you on the exciting journey ahead.

DAY 27 - OVERVIEW: THE EXCITING JOURNEY AHEAD

And that wraps-up your four-week business book.

By now, you should have a trading business, and some great plans and ideas for how you'll continue to grow this business.

I hope every step I've been through with you has been easy to follow and you've learnt something new from every book section.

I also hope you've actioned every section - even the more boring ones!

But, all of the instructions and preparation aside, and all of the tasks that come with running and growing a start-up, don't forget to never lose focus of why you started your business.

Revert back to the passion-finding exercise we did back in week 1. When things get tough, or when you feel like you're being distracted by other things, always think back to why you started the business in the first place - and it's ultimately this passion and motivation that will drive you to grow your business, it will be your anchor through the good and bad times that your business brings, so always hold this in your mind as you progress.

Also, be proud of what you've achieved to-date. A lot of people just dream of starting their own business, you've gone ahead and taken action - you now have your own business!

Ahead there will be times of excitement, struggle, accomplishment, and failure, remember to celebrate the wins and balance the negatives with the positives - after all, what's the alternative, working a 9-5?

Not for me, and I'm pretty sure you will feel the same now your own business is underway.

Good luck, and enjoy the journey!

www.ingramcontent.com/pod-product-compliance
Lightning Source LLC
Chambersburg PA
CBHW060848220526
45466CB00003B/1283